DAVIS CUP® by NEC

THE YEAR IN TENNIS 1998

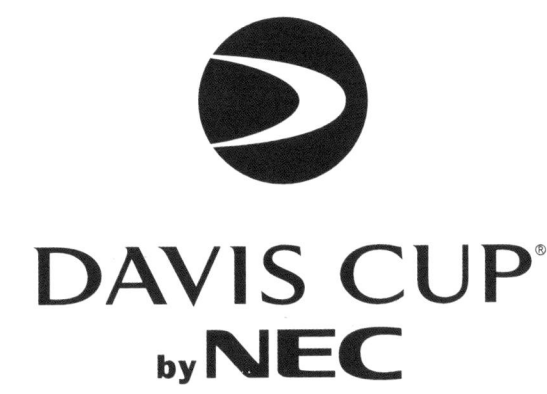

DAVIS CUP® by NEC

THE YEAR IN TENNIS 1998

TEXT BY CHRISTOPHER CLAREY

THE INTERNATIONAL TENNIS FEDERATION

UNIVERSE

First published in
the United States of America in 1999
by **Universe Publishing**
A Division of Rizzoli International
Publications, Inc.
300 Park Avenue South
New York, NY 10010

© 1999 The International Tennis
Federation
Bank Lane, Roehampton
London SW15 5X2
England

99 00 01 / 10 9 8 7 6 5 4 3 2 1

Printed in England

Designed by Derek Ungless

CONTENTS

President's message

In the ninety-ninth year of the competition, a record 131 nations entered and Sweden once again underlined its status as the number-one nation. However, the Davis Cup by NEC proved once again that it is about far more than numbers, impressive though they are.

A look at the photographs in this book, taken by some of the best photographers in the business, shows that this is a competition about passion, meaning, pressure, emotion, and giving your all for team and country. The accompanying words by Christopher Clarey explore the reasons, motivations, and actions that inspired these emotional highs and lows.

The highs and lows have included Spain's dramatic triumph over Brazil; Zimbabwe's giant-killing feat against Australia; Sweden's backs-to-the-wall fight back against the Slovak Republic; Italy's surprise defeat of the USA; and Sweden's triumph in Milan. Since the World Group was introduced in 1981, Sweden has won six titles and reached eleven finals. This dominance has been based on teamwork, fighting spirit, and a never-say-die attitude—plus some very talented individuals—all qualities of which Dwight Davis himself would have approved.

We hope you enjoy the 1998 Davis Cup Yearbook. Chris Clarey has undertaken considerable original research and one-on-one interviews which have brought to life this year's competition.

Next year is a special one for the competition, as we celebrate one hundred years of Davis Cup. A year-long program of celebrations is planned and will be fronted by some of the great names of the competition—Vijay Amritraj, Boris Becker, Stefan Edberg, John Newcombe, Yannick Noah, Nicola Pietrangeli, and Stan Smith—who will be acting as Davis Cup Centenary ambassadors.

My congratulations go to the champions, Sweden, and to Italy, as gallant runners-up. I look forward to the 1999 Davis Cup and the competition to be crowned champion nation in the centenary year.

Brian Tobin, President, International Tennis Federation

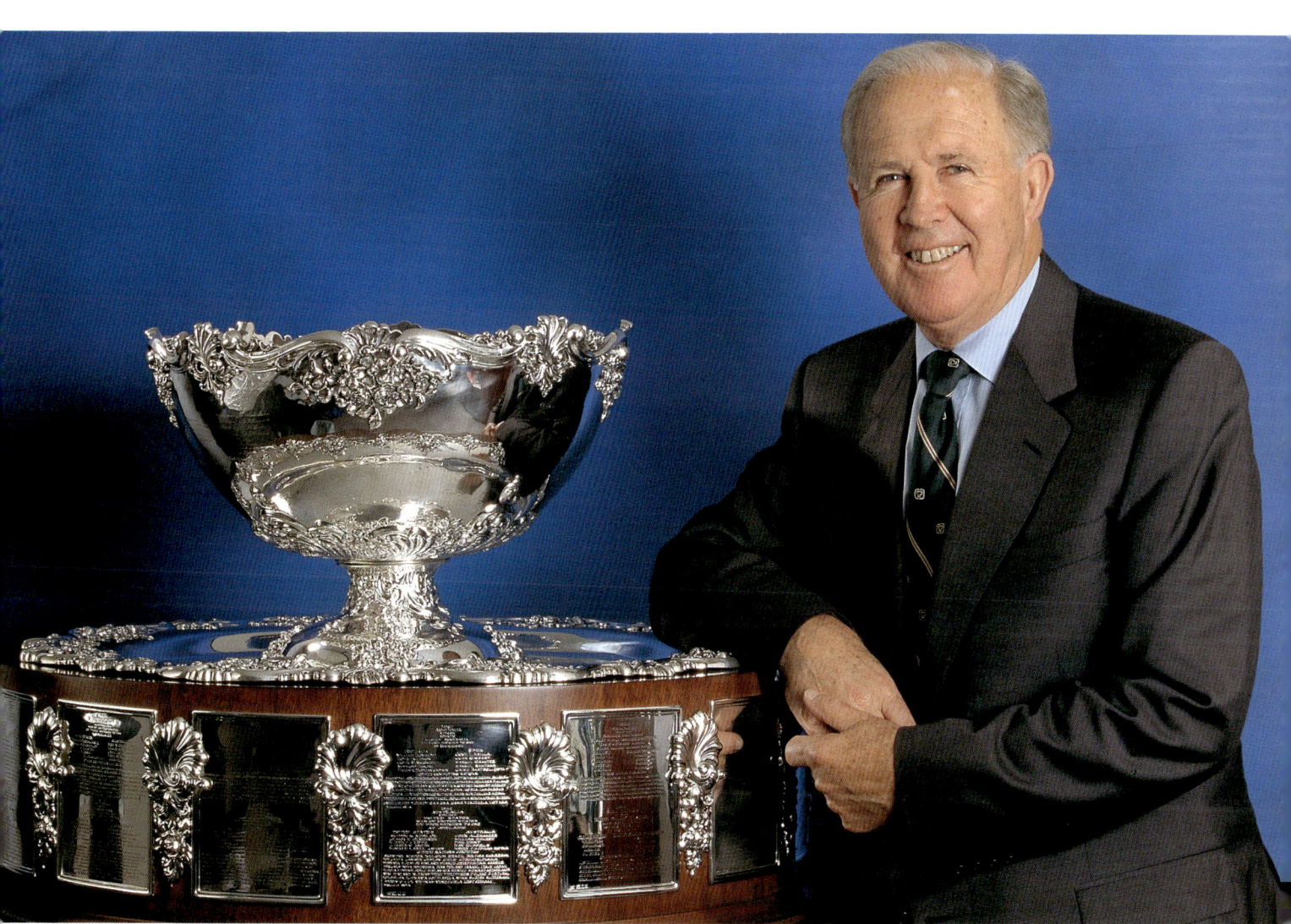

Foreword

I remember 1985 very well. It was the year that I won my first Grand Slam singles title at Wimbledon and the year I began to play Davis Cup for Germany. In March of that year, months before I played Wimbledon as a seventeen year old, I was very proud to be nominated to represent my country in their opening round tie against Spain. We played at home, at Sindelfingen. Although I was somewhat nervous, I started off well with a fairly easy win over Juan Aguilera and then teamed with Andreas Maurer to play one of the best doubles teams of that time, Sergio Casal and Emilio Sanchez. Maurer and I were down two sets to one against the Spanish but we were able to come back, with our victory deciding the tie in the fifth set. It was an incredible feeling to win for your country, something I had never experienced before but which I never forgot.

Our victory over Spain put Germany on course to reach its first Davis Cup Final in December of that year. A lot was expected of me and of our team, but we weren't able to win the 1985 title. A very good team from Sweden, with another young player named Stefan Edberg, was a little bit better than we were that weekend and defeated us in the fifth rubber. It was disappointing, but the loss made us even more determined. We had to wait a little while but we had our revenge, winning the Davis Cup title over Sweden in 1988 and 1989.

Many things have happened since those days, including the reunification of my country. Personally I have been very fortunate to have had great success in my life, both on the court and off. There are lots of good memories for me, with some of the most vivid ones coming from Davis Cup. I have come to appreciate the competition more as I have become older, and the special qualities that it takes to play and win for your country.

Two of the most extraordinary moments for me came when playing outside of Germany and both taught me a little bit more about myself. In 1987, in the Relegation Round against United States in Hartford, I had to call upon every resource in my arsenal to defeat John McEnroe in the second rubber. The match, which was five sets and six hours and twenty-one minutes long, was so emotional for both John and me. The crowd was clearly in John's corner and there is no more dedicated Davis Cup player than John. I was lucky enough to win that day and had enough left to come back out on Sunday and defeat Tim Mayotte, again in five sets, to secure the win for Germany. It was an exhilarating and draining experience for me but it also made me grow as a player and as an individual. It was a defining moment in my career. More difficult for me than playing myself was to sit injured on the sidelines in Moscow in the 1995 semifinals and watch my teammate Michael Stich lose the fifth rubber to Andrei Chesnokov. Michael, who also played well in Davis Cup, had nine match points but couldn't put it away. The anguish that he felt in losing was shared by all of us on the team. It is an image that has stayed with me for a long time.

This past year I have been a part of a new German team, featuring our two young talents, Nicolas Kiefer and Tommy Haas. I have made my contributions on the court in the doubles but I have also tried to impart to them my love for the Davis Cup and the rewards that come from being part of a team that plays for its country.

I wish my team had been able to go all the way to the Final, but we were stopped in the quarterfinals by another very committed team from Sweden. The example set by the Swedes in this competition is that of esprit de corps. The Swedish teams of the 1980s and 1990s understand, I believe, the true spirit of the Davis Cup. As a team, they fight for each victory and they make sacrifices to win. It is important to the Swedes to be the Davis Cup champions. Other nations can learn from them how effective total commitment to a cause can be. I congratulate them on another very successful year. I caution them, however, that there is always next year and we will be waiting for them with a view to another Davis Cup title for Germany.

Davis Cup will be one hundred years old in 1999 and has grown from an idea into one of the world's most important sporting events. It makes me proud to know that my country is one of only nine to have won this great title and that my name is carved on the trophy with the legends of the game that I love.

Boris Becker

A crossroads with conflicting signs

WHAT WOULD DWIGHT DAVIS have made of his Cup in 1998?

As a competitive man, he clearly would have enjoyed the return to the elite of Great Britain, the nation whose once-piquant rivalry with his own inspired him to create the event.

As a well-educated man with an interest in international affairs, he certainly would have appreciated the burgeoning depth in men's tennis: the revival of Belgium; the emergence of Zimbabwe and the Slovak Republic.

As a philanthropist and sportsman, he certainly would have approved of and related to the mutual support demonstrated by Sweden's players as they urged each other on to another collective success.

But as a former secretary of war and civic-minded American, Davis would certainly have been troubled, even embarrassed, by the absence of his countrymen Pete Sampras, Andre Agassi, and Michael Chang in the star-crossed semifinal against Italy on American territory.

As a man raised on newspapers and radio, he also would have been perplexed by the increasingly earnest and edgy debate about making his venerable event more palatable to television: a sociological phenomenon that was not yet dominating living rooms and driving discussions during his lifetime.

Davis Cup already has been through major transformations: it has gone from a two-nation, transatlantic garden party to a sprawling, global event with 129 nations entered in the competition for 1999, its centenary year. It has gone from the challenge round to an open draw; from an open draw to a sixteen-team World Group. It has gone from an exclusively outdoor event to an event that is often held indoors; from an event open only to amateurs to an event in which professionals are paid a significant sum and no longer get much rest between the third and fourth sets.

But now, after a muted 1998 Davis Cup season that peaked early and petered out anticlimactically in a lopsided if well-attended Final in Milan, more major change is again under discussion, and not just among outsiders with no clout or vote. Should Davis Cup be a more compact competition at the top with only fourteen teams in the World Group or with one less round per year in order to encourage top players to participate? Should it opt for best-of-three-set

The Davis Cup, donated by Harvard student Dwight Davis one hundred years ago, underwent some refurbishment in 1998 in advance of the competition's Centenary year. Silversmiths Shreve Crump & Low of Boston, who created the original trophy with Reed & Barton, polished the Cup for its birthday and added a redesigned, wider second plinth.

singles matches instead of best-of-five to help promote television coverage? Should there be no-ad scoring? Should it encompass two days instead of three?

Or should Davis Cup, as Australian captain John Newcombe and German star Boris Becker suggested, simply be left well enough alone?

"The root of the problem in tennis is not too much Davis Cup," Becker said. "The root of the problem is too much tennis."

Becker's point is well taken, as a cursory glance at the men's 1999 schedule will quickly confirm. In a glut, quality is what usually holds sway. Would it not be wiser to trim the fat instead of the meat?

"We played a relegation match last year in Townsville, which is way up on the north coast of Australia," Newcombe said. "It is a city of 120,000 people, not a big place, and we had a 4,800-seat stadium for a match against Uzbekistan, which does not make it a major match in Australia. We sold out every day and even on day three when we were up 3–0 there was not an empty seat in the house. For me, that's a sign that Davis Cup is very healthy in our part of the world."

But as robust as Davis Cup might be in Australia and as popular as two-time U.S. Open champion Patrick Rafter remains, the Australian team had problems of its own in 1998. There was a stunning first-round loss to Zimbabwe and, more symptomatic of this era where individual and collective interests are not always in harmony, a major defection in the imposing form of Mark Philippoussis.

Philippoussis, who declined to play because of a disagreement with Newcombe and Australian Davis Cup coach Tony Roche, was one of seven members of the year-end top 20 who did not play Davis Cup at all in 1998. Two were Spaniards—Felix Mantilla and Albert Costa—who were not asked to play. But Philippoussis, Sampras, Australian Open champion Petr Korda, Richard Krajicek, and Goran Ivanisevic, who had a conflict with the Croatian federation, would have been welcome additions to their teams.

"I really believe that very early in the next millennium we should make some changes in this format to make it more user friendly, more fan friendly, more player friendly," said American captain Tom Gullikson. "We need to make it a better product to give to the people because, let's face it, it doesn't do Davis Cup any good when the best players aren't playing."

Newcombe does not argue with Gullikson's thesis that player commitment is vital but he does differ on the degree of the problem and the solution: "What you should do if you really want to see if Mr. Davis's Cup is alive and well is see how many leading players do not play from the 129 countries who compete," he said. "In 90 to 95 percent of those countries, I bet they do play, and if I'm correct, the guys who do not play, particularly the guys from the USA, need to have a hard look at themselves and what they stand for. Do they stand for their own interests and money or do they stand for the history of the game?"

Newcombe is correct about participation levels internationally, but the irony is that Sampras does draw inspiration from the history of the game. He pushed himself hard in the autumn of 1998 in a successful attempt to become the first man to finish number one in the rankings six years in a row. Although he surprisingly withdrew from the 1999 Australian Open, citing mental and physical fatigue, he presumably will push himself again in an attempt to surpass Roy Emerson's career record of twelve Grand Slam singles titles. But Davis Cup, despite its century of existence and despite the fact that it is older than the Australian Championships or the all-comers French championships (only French club members competed until 1925), does not have the same hold on Sampras's priorities or on his country.

Californians, Floridians, and Long Islanders still make a habit of talking about Wimbledon and the U.S. Open on the beach and around their barbecues. But the Davis Cup rarely gets the same treatment.

"It's just different," Sampras said. "I've been part of a couple of winning teams, and the impact in the States, really, there isn't much of one. You don't feel like the Ryder Cup team when they win it."

Outgoing U.S.T.A. president Harry Marmion, who made Davis Cup a priority during his two-year tenure but failed to bring the trophy home, believes "there is too much money available in a crass commercial way to players; they don't need Davis Cup. But the other problem is that the American public doesn't have as strong a feeling about Davis Cup as I would like them to have.

"The root of the problem is too much tennis," said Becker. John Newcombe agrees.

Centenary ambassadors Boris Becker of Germany (opposite) and John Newcombe of Australia (above) are staunch and vocal supporters of the Davis Cup. Other Centenary ambassadors are Vijay Amritraj of India, Stefan Edberg of Sweden, Yannick Noah of France, Nicola Pietrangeli of Italy, and Stan Smith of the United States.

There are too many alternatives for them: too much going on in other sports."

What is clear is that Sampras's palpable lack of passion for the event does not help Davis Cup's cause in his homeland. True, tennis was a more popular and fashionable diversion in the United States when John McEnroe lifted Davis Cup out of the doldrums by committing himself to it in the 1970s and 1980s, but McEnroe's interest in the event unquestionably trickled down to the public, which was interested in McEnroe.

"America is driven by the star system," Gullikson said. "Somebody says, 'Hey let's go to a movie.'" And the first thing you ask is, 'Who's in it?' If your recognize one of the names without knowing the story line, you say, 'OK.' We are very used to that, and if you ask, 'Who's playing?' and it's Todd Martin, number 25 in the world, people wonder why they can't watch Agassi or Sampras."

The question is whether it makes sense to restructure Davis Cup in a potentially vain attempt to shore up the American market and appeal to a generation of American stars whose halcyon days are numbered and whose national federation already has committed to inculcating more civic spirit in the next generation of players it helps develop.

"I find it a little bit strange that some of the American guys didn't grow up watching more Davis Cup," said Swedish captain Carl-Axel Hageskog. "But there's no way you can change Davis Cup and make it different in Sampras's mind. Even if you play every second year, he will have the same view of it anyway. I think it's stupid to give away the advantages of the tradition and history of Davis Cup because of one or two or three players."

Davis Cup does remain strong in much of Europe, large swathes of South America, and Australia, but Todd Martin, one of the Cup's staunchest supporters in the United States, worries that recalcitrance could prove contagious at the top, and for that reason he advocates playing the Davis Cup over a two-year period with two rounds each year: "I think guys will feel the pressure if they see what Pete's done and they will perhaps say that this is what you have to do to be number one," Martin said. "Unfortunately, it probably does help Pete, relative to his goal, not to play Davis Cup."

Sampras, who has suggested that Davis Cup be played every two years, is hardly the first star to decline. All the Swedes might be eager to play Davis Cup in the late 1990s, but when Bjorn Borg was dominating tennis in the late 1970s, he refused to play on occasion to concentrate on personal goals. American star Jimmy Connors did the same, as (lest we forget) did Becker when he was actively and successfully pursuing the number-one ranking.

"Sure, but you are talking about a very small group of players," said Becker, who, like Sampras, won the competition twice before sitting it out. "No one right now can compare themselves with Pete. He is trying to beat Emerson's record. You're talking about the best ever. That's a position not many players will ever be in.

"Of course it would be very important to everybody if Pete plays in 1999, but he's the one who obviously has to make up his mind. If the scheduling would be such that he would have enough time to follow his pursuits on the regular tour, he would play. He played before; but in the end it is just one player, and Davis Cup is bigger than one player."

Becker, like most European players and captains with the notable exception of Swedish star Jonas Bjorkman, believes Davis Cup should remain an annual event. The ITF and its president, Brian Tobin, an Australian, also show no interest in public in the biennial concept and very little interest in Martin's two-rounds-per-year proposal.

"I don't think that's got much favor at all," Tobin said of the biennial approach. "Would you play the ATP Finals every second year? You wouldn't, would you? You need continuity."

You also need revenue, and voluntarily reducing the length of Davis Cup would, at least in the short term, reduce the value of contracts with sponsors. That would affect the funding provided to the national federations, who rely heavily on Davis Cup. In Zimbabwe, a nation with a struggling economy and no tour events, Davis Cup revenue and the sponsorship associated with it account for 90 percent of the federation's annual budget.

"We wouldn't agree with the biennial idea at all," said Paul Chingoka, president of Zimbabwe's tennis association. "We are starved for international tennis anyway."

But Tobin and the ITF's Davis Cup Committee, which includes Marmion, Australia's Neale Fraser, and Spain's Juan Margets, are clearly more open to experimentation than in recent years.

Two American players, two very different views of the Davis Cup.

Two Americans with two very different views of the Davis Cup: Pete Sampras (opposite), who has played on two winning teams but who declined to play for his country in 1998, and John McEnroe (above), who played Davis Cup for the United States for a record twelve years and won more singles matches than any other American.

Two changes that appear likely are the introduction of a fifth-set tiebreaker and the introduction of computer points for Davis Cup when the ATP Tour changes its ranking system in the year 2000. There has been rapprochement between the ITF and ATP of late, and the advent of ranking points might encourage participation in Davis Cup and would certainly not discourage it, although it will create inequities elsewhere (top players whose nations are not in the World Group and top players who are not quite good enough to make their teams could suffer slightly in the rankings).

But personal experience and concerns about television coverage are encouraging more radical thinking, too. Tobin believes the attention spans of the remote-control-wielding youth of today are simply not equipped to deal with nine hours of singles play on an opening Friday, and, frankly, he is no longer certain that his own attention span is equipped to deal with it.

"I think people at the matches are getting a little tired of sitting there for hours, particularly if we are out in the sun somewhere watching the same two guys play," he said. "It's not just television. I think we need to present a better product to the public."

"I think we're going to experiment at least with three-set matches in Davis Cup," he added.

The question is where such an experiment might take place. The two lowest divisions of Davis Cup, the customary testing ground, already play best-of-three-set tennis. It is only in the top three divisions—the World Group, Group One, and Group Two—that best-of-five is used.

Group Two would seem the most likely and least invasive spot for a test run, but most Group Two matches are not televised, so how useful a test would it be? What programmers dislike about best-of-five is the huge disparity in match lengths, and although there is considerable disparity in best-of-three, the time window is smaller and apparently more manageable.

One of the proposals the Davis Cup Committee is seriously considering putting before the ITF is best-of-three singles matches in the first two rounds and best-of-five-set doubles matches throughout so that doubles can continue to be showcased.

"A good three-set singles match that's close and swings both ways can be just as good as a five-set match," said Fraser, a longtime player and captain for Australia whose resistance to shortening Davis Cup singles matches has slowly melted. "I'm seeing the other side of the coin sitting in these meetings, and television is definitely loudly and clearly saying that we'd love to broadcast Davis Cup but unless you can give us some approximate time it will be on for, it's hard to sell."

The flip side of the coin is that selling significant change to people inside the game is going to be difficult. Any alteration in Davis Cup's format must be approved by a two-thirds majority of the ITF members at the organization's annual meeting, although concerns about diminishing television revenue certainly could serve as a spur in the flank of reform. According to Newcombe, the Davis Cup captains who attended meetings with the ITF at Wimbledon and the U.S. Open in 1998 were unanimously opposed to reducing to best-of-three; he said they were also opposed to the introduction of no-ad scoring.

"If you cut to best-of-three, it's not a heavyweight championship anymore," Hageskog said. "I think a lot of excitement comes with the five sets."

Davis Cup has provided a great deal of excitement in the last ninety-nine years. It provided some more in 1998, although most of the thrills came early instead of late. The majority of the game's greatest players—from the Doherty brothers to Bill Tilden to Rod Laver to Borg to Sampras—have put their names on the silver punchbowl that Davis commissioned. That punchbowl is a work in progress, as the tasteful redesign it recently underwent made clear, but what recent history has also underscored is that the competition the punchbowl symbolizes remains a work in progress, too.

The tough question in this historic year is what that competition needs more: renovation or conservation?

ROUND ONE

Nyama Yekugocha! Roasting the hosts

THE *LINGUA FRANCA* IN MILDURA, Australia, during the first round of the 1998 Davis Cup was English. It is the language of the Black brothers, Byron and Wayne, and, with a few variations, the language of the Australians. But to understand what the logic-twisting result represented to the Blacks' country, it was helpful to speak at least a bit of Shona.

"Yave Nyama Yekugocha!" sang Paul Chingoka, the president of Zimbabwe's Tennis Association, as he stood triumphantly and a little unsteadily in the stands in Mildura.

"Yave Nyama Yekugocha!" sang the hundreds of fans who were dancing on the airport tarmac in the Zimbabwean capital of Harare when the first of the Black brothers flew home from Perth.

"Yave Nyama Yekugocha!" is the refrain to a Shona song that is traditionally performed after a hunt. Literally, it means "The meat is ready for roasting," and what it really means is that the hunt has been successful.

What made the singing on both continents all the more powerful and poignant was that hardly anyone from Zimbabwe expected such an outcome. It was enough that the Zimbabwean team had qualified for the World Group for the first time in its nation's history. When the draw for 1998 was unveiled, the Blacks were staring at what looked like an unscalable peak: a first-round road trip to face the Australians on grass.

This was the same Australian team, led by captain John Newcombe and coach Tony Roche, that was intent on prying the Cup loose from Europe and transporting it down under to one of its traditional resting places; the same Australian team that had Patrick Rafter, the reigning U.S. Open singles champion, and one of the most successful doubles teams in history in Mark Woodforde and Todd Woodbridge.

It all sounded imposing enough to dissuade even the public television channel in Zimbabwe, which elected not to commit the resources to broadcast the matches live or even with a short delay to allow for the multiple-hour time difference. "Everyone was convinced we were just going there to fulfill a duty, and there was no way it was going to be a David and Goliath affair," Chingoka said.

As it turned out, David did win, but not until Goliath experienced some downsizing.

First came Mark Philippoussis's refusal to make himself available for selection. Then, in the week preceding the tie, came his accusation that Newcombe and Roche had not supported him sufficiently during his father's recent bout with cancer. That outburst would provide Australia and its best players with conversational fodder for much more than the week of Davis Cup. What made it even more difficult to fathom and forget was Philippoussis's perplexing and ultimately unsuccessful attempt at damage control: he came to Mildura anyway, racquets in hand, to watch instead of lead his former teammates into the second round.

It was all a major and extremely well-documented distraction, but if Philippoussis, then ranked 16th in the world, had been the only item to go awry on the checklist, the once-harmonious

The younger Black, Wayne, for the first time outranked older brother Byron and played number-one singles for Zimbabwe. Preceding pages: Australia played its first Davis Cup tie of 1998 before a sellout crowd at Mildura, Victoria, which marked the first time Davis Cup had been played outside one of Australia's state capital cities.

Australians still might have found a way to dominate the team they already dominated in the computer rankings. Unfortunately for the Aussies' sense of manifest destiny, there would be other snafus. Even their own grass would work against them: it grew straight up instead of at an angle, producing a truer, higher bounce quite favorable to Zimbabwean baseliners with good returns.

Health was a bigger problem. Although able to play, Woodbridge was still recovering from a virus, and Rafter, who had a virus of his own, had not yet begun the recovery process. "He had caught something during the European indoor season, and when he came back to Australia for Davis Cup, he had a vaccination because he was going to India soon, and the next day he just came down with it," Newcombe said. "When we traveled to Mildura on Saturday, he was walking like he had cramps all over his body. The thing had just invaded his muscles."

Rafter would spend much of the next four days in bed, and when he finally decided to play, he was far from his swashbuckling self. At this point, Rafter had not yet had a 1998 to remember—he was struggling with his form and new superstar status—and his fortunes were not to improve in this inland country town in Victoria despite the full support of a sellout crowd that was delighted Mildura had been chosen over Australia's more cosmopolitan metropolises.

Until now, all Davis Cup ties in Australia had been held in state capitals, but the Australian tennis trust's plan was to spread the wealth and word in 1998. If all went swimmingly, they would have four home ties in the same year—"we had an unbelievable draw," Newcombe said—and work was already moving ahead in Brisbane to prepare for the quarterfinal that was expected to follow. But Brisbane would have to wait, because Davis Cup was about to live up to its well-deserved reputation as an event where a surprise should not really come as a surprise. Nationalism—and all the particular pressures that accompany it—is a powerful equalizer on a tennis court.

In the months leading up to the tie, the Blacks' plucky Australian coach Brett "Moose" Stephens had been making mischievous comments to his countrymen like, "High Noon, Mildura."

Byron and younger brother Wayne had reached the World Group by upsetting Thomas Muster and the Austrians in Harare's indoor stadium six months earlier. Wayne had won the decisive fifth rubber and was quickly bowled over by Byron and then buried by several other members of Zimbabwe's very small but tightly connected tennis clique. "The cherry on the top was our tennis president, a pretty big guy, who just jumped on top of the pile and squashed the last bit of air out of us," Byron said. "It was pretty touching all around."

Chingoka knew what an opportunity the World Group was in a country of limited economic means, with shallow tennis roots and only a small amount of topsoil. To underscore it, he decided to make a direct plea to the Australians that they ignore the luck of the draw, surrender their home-court advantage and allow the Zimbabweans to host their first tie among the elite.

"It was a serious offer and the reason was that our tennis fraternity never had the chance to watch anybody in the top 20 except Thomas Muster and I wanted the Australians to give us a chance to watch tennis at that level," Chingoka said.

Australians are generally a fair-minded lot, but largesse has its limits, and the tie remained on the Aussies' home court. Byron was concerned that his president's well-intentioned request had sent the wrong signal. "At the time, I thought it was a bit foolish; you sort of want to keep your guard up a little bit," Byron said. "I don't think he expected us to win himself. Maybe that's why he said it."

Appearances and national mood to the contrary, the Australian players were aware that the Blacks were more dangerous than the numbers by their names (both were ranked in the 80s). "If their sister plays, too, we are in all sorts of trouble," Rafter joked, referring to Cara, the world's top-ranked junior in 1997.

"People at home think Australia is so strong we should crush the Zimbabweans, but Byron Black has been around many years," Woodforde said shortly before the tie. "He is a tremendous, hard-fighting, gritty player who won't ever give up, and his brother Wayne is turning out the same. They don't have height on their side and maybe lack a bit of strength, but they make up for it with guts."

A taller yet smaller man

Few have accused the strapping six-foot-four-inch Philippoussis of lacking strength—at least not the muscular variety. It was Newcombe who coined the nickname "Scud" for Philippoussis, and for much of his brief career, the man-child from Melbourne had been all too true to that sobriquet: generating plenty of sparks, attracting plenty of attention, and, despite some direct hits on important targets, failing to perform up to expectations or design specifications.

Davis Cup absentees meet with little resistance in the United States these days, but Australia still exacts a higher toll on its defectors. "I wouldn't say it's treason, but it's a big deal," Newcombe said. "I'm very sad Mark isn't playing, and I hope it gets fixed because in the four years before this, we've had a very good relationship with him."

When Philippoussis originally told Newcombe he would not be available to face Zimbabwe, the reason given was that he wanted to spend more time with his family. But when his comments were published in the Melbourne daily, the *Herald Sun*, in the days leading up to the tie, his real reasons were suddenly as clear as the summer sky over Ayers Rock. Philippoussis felt rejected. "Of course I understand how dear the Davis Cup is, but if someone has done wrong by me, I don't forget easily," he said. "Being of Greek and Italian blood, it's just me; just the way we are." Philippoussis also wanted a public apology from Newcombe: "He should go out there and say it. Why not? What has he got to hide because he knows he's wrong?"

Not surprisingly, Newcombe, an Australian icon and tennis icon long before the twenty-one-year-old Philippoussis was born, had a radically different take. In his mind, he had nothing to apologize for. "I've got a file of probably sixteen letters I've faxed to Mark during the last five years," he said. "And if you read that file, you would definitely say this is someone who is a very good friend of Mark's. That's how I feel."

For Philippoussis, the problems had begun the previous September, when the Australian team lost to the Americans in the 1997 Davis Cup semifinals in Washington D.C. Philippoussis had been part of that squad but had played oddly muted tennis. Consistency has never been and probably never will be Philippoussis's hallmark—not with his appetite for risk and his flickering attention span. "He's never going to be a fifty-two-week player," his coach, Gavin Hopper, said. "But if he plays a lot of good tournaments during the season, we're going to have a great player on our hands."

Against the Americans, Philippoussis was far from great, losing to Pete Sampras and Michael Chang in singles, but with his father Nick in the midst of cancer treatments, the struggling, distracted son decided that what he needed was for Roche, a superb technician but less gifted communicator, to coach him exclusively in Europe during four tournaments in the fall.

The request was declined, in part because Roche already spends nearly half the year away from his family and because Hopper was already traveling with Phillippoussis. But according to Nick

Philippoussis, Newcombe and Roche also told him over coffee in Washington that they were not pleased with Mark's level of dedication to his training or his decision to skip Davis Cup in 1996.

"Newcombe told me Mark's ranking would go down and he would lose interest in tennis," Nick told the *Sydney Morning Herald*. "He said that perhaps Mark thinks it's good to have one Ferrari or two Ferraris and that is all he wants from tennis. He said they had decided not to coach him. I told Mark what they said and he was very upset. He thought I could be dying and all he wanted was some support with his tennis and he wasn't getting it."

Newcombe does not contest Nick's account of the meeting, but he certainly regrets calling it. "That's the one thing I would do differently," he said. Newcombe also believes he has been supportive: "I rang Nick once or twice a week every week last year when he was sick at home in Melbourne," he said. "I'm not sure how many other people did that."

Doctors declared Nick's cancer in remission in late 1997, but the condition of Mark's relationship with his former Davis Cup mentors continued to deteriorate. His decision not to play Davis Cup would also drive a wedge between himself and the Woodies and, more painfully, Rafter, his former partner in revelry and on the doubles court. In February, Rafter put an end to their partnership, and their once close friendship, which had begun unraveling the previous year, would ultimately devolve into strained cordiality.

Philippoussis's outburst and what happened in Mildura did little to reverse the slippage. Patrick Smith, a columnist for the *Sydney Morning Herald*, memorably dubbed the young star "Sillippoussis" and wrote that any attempt to win "a fight for public sympathy and understanding" against Newcombe was "remarkable in its stupidity."

Perhaps sensing this, Philippoussis's handlers and Australian politician Jeff Kennett, the Victorian premier, urged him to fly to Mildura, which happens to be in Philippousis's home state, rather than spend the weekend at his seaside house in Anglesea. Perhaps unwisely, Newcombe agreed, and Philippoussis arrived with a friend on the day of the draw.

"I had issues, and I'm not stepping away from those issues, but I'm making it positive and supporting the team," said Philippoussis, who assured his interlocutors that his presence would not be disruptive.

This was hopeful indeed. Woodforde later deemed his presence "absurd," but Philippoussis was in the stands and also in the television commentary booth when his replacement, Jason Stoltenberg, gave Australia a 1–0 lead with a four-set victory over Wayne Black that could have been a great deal more routine if Stoltenberg had not double-faulted on match point in the third set. Philippousis was also in the stands and occasionally on his cellular phone when Byron Black upset Rafter in the next match by the score of 3–6, 6–3, 6–2, 7–6 (7–0).

In truth, Rafter probably should have been sitting in the stands, as well. Byron and Rafter are quite friendly, and Byron had been ribbing Rafter that week, calling him "virus" whenever they crossed paths. According to Newcombe, Rafter was "exhausted after the first forty minutes" of Friday's match. But Rafter handled the setback with grace—not the word of the weekend in Mildura: "Obviously I was not as fit and strong as I could have been but to Byron's credit he played well," he said.

The Woodies played well themselves on Saturday, defeating the Black brothers in straight sets despite the Blacks' 10–1 record together in Davis Cup doubles. That gave Australia a 2–1 lead, but on Saturday night after a team meeting, it was decided that Woodforde would replace Rafter in the first reverse singles.

With a weapon like the Woodies—Todd Woodbridge (top left) and Mark Woodforde (top right)—Australia easily defeated Zimbabwe in the doubles. Australian hopes were centered on U.S. Open champion Patrick Rafter (bottom), but a bacterial infection hampered his effectiveness in Mildura.

"Pat would have played," Newcombe said. "In the end, Tony and I weren't prepared to risk Pat's health on it, because we knew that if he went out there he'd give it everything he had and then some. When you have that bad a virus in your body, you can do yourself some long-term damage."

Initially displeased by the late lineup change, the Blacks soon proceeded to seize their historic opportunity. First Wayne disposed of Woodforde in four sets, 6–3, 7–5, 6–7 (5–7), 6–4: only the second grass-court victory of his career as a professional.

Asked if the Australians had underestimated the opposition, Woodforde responded, "I hope Pat didn't underestimate them, or Newk and Rochey. I don't think those guys would have. I doubt Stolts would have, but maybe Mr. Philippoussis did."

It was a touch of Victorian formality in Victoria, and it was telling. "I'm just upset that I have to get called in at the last moment," Woodforde added. "I'm not angry at Pat. It was just such a short time to prepare yourself for such a big match when you've just come off the doubles."

Stoltenberg had known he was playing singles for weeks, but with Australia's season on the line, he would fare no better. Byron might not have had a virus or a grudge to bear, but he had some problems of his own: tendinitis in his left foot that the soft grass aggravated slightly.

Byron later admitted that if Zimbabwe had any other players capable of winning, he would have seriously considered pulling himself out of the lineup. "It had been niggling me for about a month before the tie, but more than the niggles, my problem was that I was in a real slump," he said.

For the first time, Wayne's ranking was actually higher than his older brother's, but by the time Byron had finished off Stoltenberg, 6–2, 3–6, 6–3, 6–4, he was feeling no pain or self-doubt.

"I think it's one of the best Davis Cup upsets in history," Byron said. "Basically, one family beat Australia in Australia."

He and Wayne had both attended John Newcombe's tennis academy in Texas as teenagers, and now they had managed to defeat Newcombe's team. "I want to cry right now," said Wayne, who would choke up in post-match interviews. "It's just magic. Magic."

For all Newcombe's aura and expertise, he and Roche have yet to make much magic since taking over for Neale Fraser in 1994. In five years, their team has lost in the first round three times and been relegated once: hardly in keeping with Australia's remarkable Davis Cup tradition. And as the team that would have been champion retreated from Mildura, another statistic must have rankled, as well. It was Philippoussis's record in singles against the Blacks: 5–0 without so much as the loss of a set.

"There's a lot of healing to be done," Woodforde said. "And it's not just going to take twenty-four hours or a weekend or a fortnight."

Healing required elsewhere, too

To be fair, Philippoussis was hardly the only fine player sitting instead of sweating on the first Davis Cup weekend of the year. Nor was Rafter the only star in need of rest and medication. When reigning champion Sweden traveled to the Slovak Republic to face a very dangerous team on an indoor clay court, it did so without its number one, Jonas Bjorkman, who was home in Sweden with the flu, or its number two, Thomas Enqvist, who was home with an injured wrist. Magnus Larsson, the most experienced Davis Cupper remaining and best Swedish clay-courter, was so diminished because of a mystery virus contracted in January in Qatar that he was only good for doubles.

The Americans hosted the Russians in Stone Mountain, Georgia, without Pete Sampras or

Australia's Jason Stoltenberg (top) won the first point of the tie but lost the decisive rubber to Zimbabwe's Byron Black (bottom) in four sets. Black's victory put Zimbabwe into its first World Group quarterfinal and jump-started him out of his slump.

Michael Chang, although they did have the newly motivated Andre Agassi. The Czechs played the Swiss in Zurich without recent Australian Open champion Petr Korda. The Indians faced the Italians in Genova without their traditional Davis Cup overachiever, Leander Paes, who had a shoulder injury. The Dutch traveled to Brussels to play Belgium without formidable doubles player Paul Haarhuis, who suffered from a wrist problem, and former Wimbledon champion Richard Krajicek.

Krajicek, who has seldom played up to his potential in Davis Cup, had one of the better excuses. His girlfriend, Daphne Deckers, had recently given birth to their first child. Sweden's doubles specialist, Nicklas Kulti, also missed the first round because he was a new father. But whatever the rationale, it was also a question of bad timing hurting the Cup once again.

Scheduling has become the bane of this competition, along with American ambivalence at the top. Playing the Davis Cup in the week immediately following a prestigious, taxing event like Key Biscayne is simply asking for absences. Five of the top 20 men in the world declined to play, and they weren't all Americans. "It definitely would be better for everyone to have a two-week gap," said Swedish captain Carl-Axel Hageskog.

In all, only six of the world's top 20 did play in the World Group first round, although this can be explained partly by the sheer number of Spaniards ranked in the top 20—three of whom (Felix Mantilla, Sergi Bruguera, and Alberto Berasategui) were not selected to play—and partly because new number one Marcelo Rios and his native Chile, along with Great Britain and France, were not in the World Group at all. The only ties where full strength was matched against full strength were played in Germany, which hosted South Africa, and in Brazil, which hosted Spain.

Boris Becker: doubles specialist

The two nations making their World Group debuts in 1998 were Zimbabwe and the Slovak Republic, but the first round was also an inaugural of sorts for Germany, which had a new generation of players and new generation of administrators in team manager Boris Becker and his friend and hand-picked captain Carl-Uwe Steeb.

Becker, one of the finest Davis Cup singles players in history with a career record of 38–3, had retired from Grand Slam competition in 1997 and been handed control of Davis Cup later that year by the German Tennis Federation. But Becker's athletic career was not yet over, and he seriously flirted with the idea of playing singles against a potentially dangerous South African team led by Wayne Ferreira. Instead, Becker settled for doubles and clinched the victory for Germany with partner David Prinosil by defeating David Adams and Ellis Ferreira 5–7, 6–4, 6–4, 6–3.

"I'm pleased with my own performance, but the most important thing is that we won as a team," Becker said.

In truth, the real stars in the northern city of Bremen were twenty-year-old Cup rookies Nicolas "Kiwi" Kiefer and Tommy Haas. Davis Cup indoctrinations are seldom straightforward, but Kiefer defeated Grant Stafford in five sets in the opening rubber. Haas, who had the tougher task, then beat Ferreira in four sets. Considering Ferreira's 30–9 record in Davis Cup, it was a particularly impressive performance, and Haas, who spent more time in Florida than Germany as a teenager, also defeated Stafford in the final match to finish off the 5–0 sweep.

"We were not sure how Tommy and Kiwi would behave," Steeb said. "We knew they had the talent. Now we know they also have the temperament to play in the Davis Cup."

Opposite: Boris Becker (top left) is still one of Germany's best-loved sporting heroes. The new generation Germans are Tommy Haas (top right) and Nicolas Kiefer (bottom left) who, teamed with David Prinosil and Becker (bottom right), hoped for another Davis Cup title. South Africa's Wayne Ferreira (above) had an uncharacteristically poor showing against Germany.

"Germany is back on the map of the tennis world," Becker said grandiosely and, as the next round would make clear, rather prematurely.

The shouting stops in Brazil

Spain has been squarely on the map throughout the 1990s, and with a gifted and versatile player like Carlos Moya, they may stake out more territory in the next century, too. But Davis Cup has long been a blot on the Spanish record. They have never won it and have rarely threatened to win it. And with the overemphasis on clay in the Barcelona area, where the bulk of the Spaniards live and train, ties on the road have proved treacherous for the closely knit group currently in power.

The Spaniards would not have to worry about playing indoors or on grass when they traveled to Brazil, homeland of reigning French Open champion Gustavo Kuerten. The Brazilians are just as fond of clay as the Spaniards. But Moya and teammate Alex Corretja would have to worry about the Brazilian fans: among the world's most exuberant and destabilizing.

Davis Cup sites may change—this time, the Brazilians were in the southern coastal city of Porto Alegre—but the crowd noise is always turned up high, often controversially high, inside the confines of their stadiums. In 1992 and 1993, there were official protests about fans' behavior from the visiting Germans and Italians. In 1996 in São Paulo, Austria's Thomas Muster walked off the court during the doubles rubber of a World Group Qualifying match and refused to finish the fifth set because of the crowd's antics. In 1997, the Americans stayed long enough to win in Ribeirão Preto but not without leaving in a huff. "I've never wanted to beat a country so badly in my life," said Jim Courier, who defeated the then-little-known Kuerten in the decisive rubber.

The Brazilians, who never have been sanctioned officially, will tell you that their fans are simply expressing enthusiasm, and in theory, the Spaniards and Brazilians were on very friendly terms. But shortly after the Spaniards arrived, Brazil's intense and soon-to-be former captain, Paulo Cleto, tinkered with the tone. "We were friends until yesterday," he said. "And we will be friends again after we qualify for the next round."

It was a bold and very nearly accurate prediction. This was a first round brimming with memorable, marathon ties, and this one was certainly on the short list. The opening rubber matched the reigning French Open champion against the young man who would later take his place in the record books. Moya, who in June would be the new *roi* of Roland Garros, won the first two sets with surprising ease, but after failing to convert a break point in the fourth game of the third set, he let the suddenly revitalized Kuerten and his myriad fans into the match. "When I came on the court, I forgot something very important: the atmosphere depends on the players, not the other way around," Kuerten said.

The slender, emotive Brazilian, with coach Larri Passos and teammate Fernando Meligeni pointing at their hearts, would win the final three sets 6–4, 6–4, 6–4. His triumph certainly did not make life on-court any easier or quieter for Corretja, who managed to rally from a two-set-to-one deficit to defeat Meligeni.

On Saturday, Kuerten and partner Jaime Oncins faced Corretja and Javier Sanchez. Doubles has not been a Spanish strength since Javier's older brother Emilio was playing with Sergio Casal, and this tie was not about to shore up that weakness. "It's good, I made myself lots of new friends," Javier joked after coming off court. The Brazilians had won in four more emotional sets to give themselves

Gustavo Kuerten (top), Jaime Oncins with Kuerten (middle), and Fernando Meligeni (bottom) gave Spain a scare . . .

a 2–1 lead heading into Sunday's reverse singles: Corretja vs. Kuerten and Moya vs. Meligeni.

The matches were to begin at 10 a.m., and when Corretja walked into the stadium to practice at 8:30, nearly all of the eight thousand seats already were occupied.

"When Alex started to practice, it was already like a carnival," said Spain's captain Manuel Santana. "My main advice to Alex was not to get upset whatever the crowd said to him, and believe me, they were using some pretty bad words. We knew it was going to be a very, very difficult match."

Despite the constant harassment and constant applause for his errors, it was not all that difficult initially as Corretja took a 5–0 lead. He would win the first two sets, although Kuerten had a set point in the second. But then Kuerten began to apply the sort of quick-striking baseline pressure from both wings that makes him so formidable on clay. The Brazilian would win the third, but at 4–4 in the fourth set, he lost his nerve and serve. Corretja then held to even the tie at 2–2.

Brazil had lost its grip on a minor upset; Moya played focused, relentless tennis to defeat Meligeni in straight sets, and the Spaniards were able to celebrate on court and off with a mixture of joy and relief.

"I think Moya and Corretja were very strong in their heads, and I think that was the difference," Santana said. "It was one of the most important wins we had for Spain for many, many years."

Two months later, as the two close friends, Moya and Corretja, traded groundstrokes and slaps on the back in the final of the French Open in Paris, it was clear that the experience had also led to some more personal rewards.

"It gave me a lot of confidence for later, that final match," Moya said. "I didn't know right away that it would help me, but it changed my mentality a little bit. It proved to me that I could be a winner."

What the Brazil tie proved to the Spanish tennis public was that the Brazilians were not gracious hosts, and when Kuerten walked on court at the Real Tenis Club de Barcelona for an ATP event ten days later, the crowd returned the favor. At the hotel buffet the night before, according to French reporter Alain Deflassieux, Kuerten and Meligeni already were throwing peanuts at each other and joking that they were preparing themselves for the fans' reaction.

But after losing to Carlos Costa and getting jeered as he walked on court and off, Kuerten was no longer in the mood to make light of the tension. "It's hard to feel that your presence is not appreciated, that you're considered a bad person," he said. "In Davis Cup there are often incidents with crowds and not only in Brazil. The Spaniards said they were insulted, but we can't control everything. All you need is a few overexcited people to make it turn bad. The Spaniards shouldn't imagine that they aren't liked in Brazil. Against any team, our crowd would have been like that."

The Spaniards' victory in Brazil earned them another round on clay against the Swiss, who defeated the Czechs 3–2. Marc Rosset accounted for all three of his nation's points, beating Daniel Vacek on day one, teaming with Lorenzo Manta to beat Martin Damm and Vacek in five sets on day two, and then defeating Bohdan Ulihrach in straight sets in the opening reverse singles on day three.

Italy also earned the right to stay on clay by defeating India 4–1. When the year began, it appeared the Italians would have to travel down under for a second round on Australia's favorite surface: grass. But after the Blacks' exploits, the Italians now had the chance to host Zimbabwe on the Zimbabweans' least favorite surface. It was a broad stroke of good fortune, and it would hardly be the last for Paolo Bertolucci's team in 1998.

. . . but Carlos Moya (top) and Alex Corretja (middle) used every weapon in their arsenal to help Spain to a victory lap.

Sweden trails! Watch out.

While the Italians stayed on a roll, the defending champion Swedes appeared ready to roll over in the Slovakian capital of Bratislava. After the first day's singles matches, they trailed 2–0 and were threatening to do a fine imitation of the French who had won the Davis Cup in 1996 and then lost in the first round the following year.

Bratislava, as Slovaks are often reminded, is not Prague. There are no historic bridges spanning the river that flows nearby; no booming tourist industry to fill up coffers and cafes; and no immediate prospect of being invited to join the European Union, thanks in part to the undemocratic bent of former prime minister Vladimir Meciar. This country is the smaller half of the Czechoslovakia that split apart amicably on the first day of 1993: a landlocked place often confused with Slovenia by foreigners and confused internally about what it hopes to become.

Slovakian captain Miloslav Mecir, the 1986 U.S. Open finalist and 1988 Olympic gold medalist, is probably the world's most recognizable living Slovak if you discount Martina Hingis, who spent only her first seven years there, and actor Paul Newman, whose mother was Slovak but whose address is not. In Bratislava, Mecir was signing more autographs than his players.

"There are so many new, little countries," Mecir said. "I think it's quite difficult for people around the world to distinguish which is which. But I don't think any businessman has done so much for the country's image lately as our tennis players."

The Czech half was always the far stronger tennis half in the years when Czechoslovakia was united and produced all-time greats like Jan Kodes, Martina Navratilova, and Ivan Lendl. When the nation split, the Czech Republic stayed in Davis Cup's elite World Group while the Slovaks had to start at the bottom. But after eleven victories over the likes of Sudan and Liechtenstein and a single loss to Egypt, Mecir's young team completed its rapid ascent from Group III to the World Group by defeating Canada in 1997.

After Karol Kucera, nearly as fluid a mover as his coach Mecir, reached the semifinals of the 1998 Australian Open in January, it became clear the Slovaks had the talent to stay awhile.

"People are really tired of hearing about politics here," said doubles player Jan Kroslak on the eve of the tie. "They never know what is coming next, and every time it's the same: all the scandals. They are trying to find something else that can make them happy. Sport helps people forget these things for a little while, and we try with our efforts to help them and help our families be happy."

There were a number of contented Slovaks after the first day's performances in the sold-out, three-thousand-seat Kongresova Hall C, which sounded and looked as if it were designed by an apparatchik. In the first match, Dominik Hrbaty, the twenty-year-old who nearly upset Pete Sampras at the 1997 Australian Open, defeated Sweden's Magnus Norman 7–6 (7–5), 4–6, 6–4, 3–6, 6–2. In the second match, Kucera, the twenty-four-year-old who did upset Sampras at the 1998 Australian Open, defeated Mikael Tillstrom 1–6, 6–1, 6–2, 6–4.

"This is better than I expected," Mecir said.

Hageskog no longer knew what to expect. After having to make do without the eighth-ranked Bjorkman, 20th-ranked Enqvist, and Kulti, he arrived in Bratislava intending to use Davis Cup rookie Norman and Davis Cup veteran Magnus Gustafsson in singles. But shortly after landing, Gustafsson felt a scratch in his throat and proceeded to spend a bedridden Monday, Tuesday, and Wednesday— one day short of Rafter's record for the round—attempting to shake a high fever. That left Hageskog

Karol Kucera (top) and Dominik Hrbaty (bottom) gave Slovak Republic a 2–0 lead against defending champion Sweden at Bratislava.

with Norman and Tillstrom, neither of whom had played a Davis Cup singles match, and Tillstrom had problems of his own, including blisters on his hand and feet. If the Slovaks had been entirely healthy, too, the suspense might have ended on Saturday, but instead of using Kucera in the doubles with Kroslak, Mecir chose to save him for singles and use Kroslak and the considerably less imposing Martin Hromec. The Swedish team of Larsson and Tillstrom might have been makeshift, but it still dominated in three sets. "I was very surprised by their choice of doubles team," Hageskog said, as unaware as most that Kucera was actually suffering from a strained hamstring. "They let us get back in the match by letting us have a very easy victory."

"Because of Kucera's injury, I decided to hold him out for the singles, because I thought that was a better chance for a victory than the doubles," Mecir explained later. "It would have been difficult for him to play both."

Gustafsson was now ambulatory enough to do some part-time work for Swedish television and interview Larsson and Tillstrom on camera. The discouraging news was that a chronic disc problem in Tillstrom's back had resurfaced during the match. When he woke up on Sunday, he was still too stiff to move effectively. If it came down to a decisive fifth rubber, the thirty-one-year-old Gustafsson would have to play.

But first, Norman would have to find a way to beat Kucera and his world-class running forehand. It required five sets and some often brilliant tennis, but at 3–4 in the final set, Kucera double-faulted at 30–15 and again at 40–30. It would not be the first or last time in 1998 that Kucera's second serve would hurt him under pressure. Four points later, the Slovak knocked a backhand wide. Norman had his break and then closed out the match, moving and competing beautifully, finishing it with a forehand volley that hit the tape and rolled over: an easy way to end a most complicated match.

"It would have been very depressing to lose two times in five sets in my first Davis Cup," Norman said.

Enter Gustafsson and Hrbaty, who is eleven years Gustafsson's junior and had spent his week training and competing, not holed up in a hotel room taking his temperature. "I think I was more scared last night because I didn't count on playing at all here," Gustafsson said on Sunday. "I was really feeling awful all week. I got tired after ten minutes on court. But I practiced for forty-five minutes yesterday, and when I woke up this morning, the doctor looked me over and said it was no problem with my health."

Perhaps the most remarkable thing about the final rubber in this tie was that neither Hrbaty nor Gustafsson got injured or ill. But Gustafsson, who held a 2–0 career edge over the Slovak, was still recovering and after they split sets, Calle Hageskog told him frankly that he did not like the way he was hanging his head between points.

"I'm resting," Gustafsson answered.

"You can't let the other player see you like that; you have to be pumped up," Hageskog said.

"I'm doing my best," said Gustafsson.

"No, you are not," said Hageskog. "I've seen you play many times."

It was the last turning point in a tortuous tie. "I was almost angry at Calle," Gustafsson said later between coughs, " Because, believe me, I was fighting out there. But I think it helped."

In the end, the difference would be Gustafsson's baroque, emphatic forehand—one of the better strokes in the sport. That forehand had carried him into the top 10 in the early 1990s before a

In the first Davis Cup tie of his career, Sweden's Magnus Norman (top) outlasted Slovak Republic's Karol Kucera (bottom) to level the tie at 2–2

series of injuries had stopped his progress. When he came off court, flushed and giddy, after his 6–2, 5–7, 7–5,7–6 (7–4) victory, his teammates formed a circle and tossed him into the air.

Not too far from the Arctic circle, Kulti and Bjorkman were celebrating next to their radios in Sweden. The tie had not been televised live at home, and so the absentees had been obliged to track Gustafsson's progress through news flashes and the text button on their televisions.

"I was jumping up and down in my house," Kulti said.

But was it really a surprise? Since the World Group began in 1981, teams have rallied to win from 0–2 on only eight occasions, but the cohesive, combative Swedes have made four of those comebacks themselves. Gustafsson already had put the finishing touch on one by beating Daniel Nestor of Canada in five sets in a final rubber in 1992.

"It's always nice to have such a comeback, but I don't know if can take any more of them; my heart is too weak," said Hageskog, whose team had, without question, earned the right to face Germany.

It was Sunday night in Bratislava, and the first round should have been drawing quickly to a close. But this long Davis Cup weekend would be longer than usual, because play would have to continue until Monday in both Brussels, where the Belgians and Dutch were tied at 2–all, and in the Georgia hills, where the Americans led the Russians 2–1.

A substitute for Mikael Tillstrom in the fifth rubber, Magnus Gustafsson (below) completed Sweden's 3–2 comeback over Slovak Republic. Opposite: A surprise victory over the Netherlands gave the Belgian team and fans (top) cause for celebration even though the Dutch fans (bottom) were as supportive as ever.

Low countries, high drama

The delay on both sides of the Atlantic was caused by rain, which the Belgians probably should have anticipated when they decided to host the Dutch outdoors in early April. This was the first tie for Dutch captain Michiel Schapers, who had replaced the retired Stan Franker after the 1997 quarterfinal loss to the United States. It was definitely the first tie for Belgian captain Koen Gonnissen, the personal coach of Johan van Herck. Gonnissen only assumed the post because the captain the players agreed on—Filip Dewulf's personal coach Gabriel Gonzalez—did not have a Belgian passport. Gonzalez was an Argentine, and he would have to wait until later in the year to get the appropriate documentation and title. He was still very much part of the team in Brussels, however.

"To be considered a half-captain is not an ideal working situation," Gonnissen said. "But in these circumstances, I couldn't expect anything else."

Only one match was played on the new, exceedingly slow, and now-soggy center court at the Primerose Club on Friday. Jan Siemerink, no clay-court master with his net-charging approach to tennis, still managed to defeat Belgium's Johan van Herck in four sets. The following day, with the skies clearer, Dewulf evened the tie by defeating Sjeng Schalken 7–5, 6–2, 7–5, but because Dewulf had played more than thirty games and been nominated for doubles, the Belgians exercised their right to postpone the doubles until Sunday.

This obscure bit of legislation was on its way to becoming a conversation piece in the first round, but the rest and relaxation did not help Dewulf and partner Libor Pimek, who were manhandled by Siemerink and Jacco Eltingh, 6–1, 6–4, 6–4. This time, the thirty-game limit had not been exceeded, and the reverse singles began but without Siemerink, who had injured his wrist.

Dewulf quickly capitalized, conceding only eight games in three sets in his victory over Cup rookie John Van Lottum. The Belgians then called on their "joker," Christophe van Garsse, to face Schalken in the decisive rubber.

"We pull him out of the hat when things get a little bit tight," Dewulf explained.

Technically, van Herck had to be injured for the Belgians to replace him with van Garsse in a live rubber. In 1997, with van Herck suffering from a sore leg, van Garsse had been called in to play the decisive match in the World Group Qualifying match against France. Despite his then world ranking of 173, he had beaten Lionel Roux to relegate Yannick Noah's team to the second division.

As improbable as it seemed, van Herck was hurting again at crunch time against the Dutch (take the Belgians' word for it), and the muscular van Garsse, now ranked 150, came rumbling to the rescue again. When darkness forced play to be stopped, the player who was once told by a doctor that he would never play again because of a knee injury led Schalken 6–4, 6–4, 3–6.

Much of the discussion in Belgium before the tie had centered on the players' revolt that led to former captain Eduardo Masso's departure, but by Monday, the focus was entirely on van Garsse. When he returned to the court Monday morning along with twenty-five hundred fans, he jumped out to a 3–0 lead. "I admit that I was already imagining myself as the winner," van Garsse said. But the 60th-ranked Schalken had something else in mind and proceeded to win six straight games.

At the changeover, Gonnissen tried to help, suggesting that van Garsse think only of the present and enjoy the moment. "Christophe told me, 'Koen, don't bother. I feel the same feeling I had against the French forming bit by bit inside of me. Wait a little bit longer. I can feel it coming; it's not far away.'"

He would break Schalken twice in the final set and when the Dutchman double-faulted on match point, Belgium was in the quarterfinals of the Davis Cup for the first time since the World Group was launched and van Garsse suddenly had plenty of company on court.

"I was born with a gift: the ability to handle pressure," van Garsse explained. "I'm as happy as I've ever been. I'm so proud this team has confidence in the world's 150th-ranked player, especially to win the final point."

The question now was whom van Garsse and Belgium would play next. Would it be Russia and its inconsistent, extremely talented star Yevgeny Kafelnikov? Or would it be the United States and the inconsistent, even more talented Andre Agassi?

Christophe van Garsse starred in Belgium's upset victory over the Netherlands.

Scaling Stone Mountain

The only other time the Russians and Americans had played was in the 1995 Davis Cup Final in Moscow, which Sampras won nearly on his own, getting help only in the doubles from Todd Martin. But Sampras has played in only two Cup ties since that reputation-burnishing performance, and his most recent effort—the 1997 Final in Sweden—ended prematurely when he suffered a calf injury in his opening singles match. In 1998, Sampras made it clear early that his priorities were elsewhere. So did Chang, who also had played in that 5–0 loss to the Swedes.

"In some ways I'm still not over it," Martin said in March of the defeat. "It's disappointing because we went over there with a better team and when you look at why it didn't happen, obviously Pete got injured but you also could look across the net and see four Swedish guys who I think were 100 percent there for each other as well as themselves. I think through the years, it's been proven that Americans don't have that same attitude."

Martin knows whereof he speaks, but with Agassi remotivated and resurgent and playing in the same Stone Mountain stadium where he won the gold medal at the 1996 Summer Olympics, the Americans were still a Davis Cup power.

"Andre has got a lot of interests other than just tennis, but when he is really focused on something, he always gives it 1000 percent," said American captain Tom Gullikson. "He is kind of an obsessive sort of guy, and right now, his obsession is tennis."

Captain Tom Gullikson's other singles player was Jim Courier, like Agassi a former number one, but unlike Agassi no threat to regain that privileged status. He arrived in the Atlanta area ranked out of the top 50 for the first time since his rookie year as a professional. Injuries were part of the explanation, but Courier has often played better for his country in recent seasons than he has for himself. After the first day of play was washed out completely by rain, he performed well enough to push the sixth-ranked Kafelnikov to five sets in Saturday's opening rubber. The weather might have been drier, but it was still chilly enough to make a Russian feel more at home than a Floridian. In the end, the Russian won, 6–2, 5–7, 6–7 (2–7), 6–4, 6–4, in a match that had more quantity than quality.

"It was a great battle, but we didn't perform our best," Kafelnikov said. "Basically Jim lost the match; I didn't win."

Courier, up 40–love on his serve at 4–5 in the final set, was quick to agree after he lost five consecutive points and the match on errors. He also lost his temper in the locker room. "I'm very disappointed to lose it with my head again," he said. "You know physically there's nothing wrong out there. You don't do what I did at 4–5, 40–0."

Agassi was sound in mind and body against Marat Safin, an eighteen-year-old who was making his Davis Cup debut and played like it. Safin was born and raised in Moscow but at age fourteen moved to Valencia, Spain, because training conditions at home were poor and because a Swiss bank agreed to help finance his training. The Swiss bank, as is often the case, had an excellent eye for value. "This kid is a future top 10 player," Gullikson said.

That opinion would be shared by many before the year ended, but Agassi never allowed the 170th-ranked Safin room to grow, winning in straight sets and in a big hurry to win his sixteenth consecutive Davis Cup match and tie Bill Tilden's venerable American record.

"It's a great accomplishment," Agassi said of the record. "Davis Cup has meant a lot to me, and I've given a lot to it."

On Sunday, Martin and Reneberg would give the Americans the lead by defeating Kafelnikov, one of the world's finest doubles players, and a still stage-struck Safin, 7–6 (7–3), 6–1, 2–6, 6–1. They picked on Safin throughout the match but could not give the weather-beaten Georgia fans a chance to see any more tennis. The doubles match had exceeded thirty games—Kafelnikov expressed visible delight as soon as it did—which meant the Russians could hop into their green van and retreat to the hotel despite the afternoon sunshine.

That did not sit well with the man assigned to be the referee at the tie, Alan Mills, who also serves that function at Wimbledon: "I feel there should be some modification to that rule," he said. "I would much prefer to see some sort of referee's discretion on it."

In Mills's and Gullikson's view, the rule was intended to help singles players recover for doubles, not the other way around. "Thirty games of doubles is actually far less stressful than thirty games of singles," Mills said. But in litigious America, there was no great outcry from the Americans about someone obeying the law.

"The Russians made the call that was right for them," Gullikson said. "They were within the rules."

Nonetheless, the omens were now on the Americans' side. In the last thirty-two rounds of Cup play, they were 19–0 after winning the doubles. The problem was that Agassi, no morning person, had to face a very sharp Kafelnikov well before noon on Monday. He would lose 6–3, 6–0, 7–6 (7–3),

An American Davis Cup supporter (top) enjoyed the visit of Andre Agassi (bottom) to Stone Mountain, Georgia, where the former number one won his Olympic gold medal in 1996.

which meant Tilden could rest in peace but his teammates could not.

"Andre plays better when he's dictating, not reacting," Gullikson said.

So does Courier, and when Safin should have been at his most nervous, he was suddenly playing with ace-smacking, groundstroke-cracking insouciance. He would win the first eight games of the match. "He was blowing me off the court," said Courier, who used to do the same to his elders when he was a teenager.

But after falling behind 4–1 and two service breaks in the second set, Courier and Gullikson had what would turn out to be a pivotal discussion.

"Gully, what can I do against this guy?" Courier asked.

"I think it's clear what you can't do," said Gully. "What you can't do is try to go toe to toe with this guy."

Their conclusion: Courier should somehow slow the pace and start bringing the 6–4 Safin forward whenever possible because his volleys were nowhere near as good as his two-handed backhand. The chipping began, and before long Courier had chipped away at Safin's advantage and rhythm. He rallied to win the second set, then dropped the third as Safin resumed serving bullets. But Courier stuck with his new gameplan and won the fourth in a hurry.

All the while, he was communing whenever possible with the nearly five thousand fans who had managed to avoid work on a Monday. He was also pushing the limits of courtesy, mocking Safin when he mishit an overhead into the bleachers and questioning line calls repeatedly.

"It was the first time in my life I felt like Jimmy Connors," Courier would say later.

But Connors was never a Davis Cup convert, and Courier has become one. That day, he would become the first American to win a fifth rubber in five sets since Chang did it against Austria in the 1990 semifinals. When it ended after nearly three hours, Courier sank to his knees and leaned back as if he had won a Grand Slam final and not simply beaten a teenager playing his first five-set match. Gullikson and Courier's teammates were soon down on the hardcourt with him.

"You know we all made an effort to be here this week; all worked hard going in and somehow managed to get the job done," Courier said. "There is no better feeling than being at the bottom of that pile. There was a whole lot of love down there."

That night Courier drove to the Atlanta airport with Martin. "Jim's not too open with his feelings," said Martin, "But you could tell that brought him some instant satisfaction. There wasn't that sarcasm or cynicism. He was happy to be where he was."

The next day in Harare, Wayne Black was even happier to be where he was when his flight from Perth landed at home. Byron was not with him; he had elected to travel to Asia to play indoor events and would play extremely well there. But some distant day, when he and his brother are telling stories to their children around an African campfire, he may regret his sound reasoning. Wayne will tell how the people dancing on the tarmac lifted him up as he stepped off the plane and carried him toward the terminal. He will tell how they kept right on carrying him through customs, which had ceased to exist; how the dancing and singing kept going in the parking lot and lasted deep into the night at the Blacks' home.

"It was the greatest moment of all," said Paul Chingoka. "The first time ever I remember where both black and white residents just mixed without realizing what color was what. Everybody was just proud to be from Zimbabwe."

It had been a very successful hunt indeed.

Yevgeny Kafelnikov (top) was joined by newcomer Marat Safin (bottom) as Russia's Davis Cup team nearly upset the Americans at Stone Mountain, Georgia.

Courier: "It was the first time in my life I felt like Jimmy Connors."

With the tie resting on his shoulders, USA's Jim Courier rebounded from two sets to one down to defeat Russia's Marat Safin and put the United States into the quarterfinals. His victory was met by cheers from the Stone Mountain fans and delight by his captain, Tom Gullikson (bottom left and middle), and the other members of his team (bottom right).

Byron Black

HE GREW UP NEAR HARARE on twenty-five acres that had four grass courts and various African animals roaming the property. "We were raised in a little sort of sanctuary," Byron Black said.

It was a place that fostered an elemental connection with nature and with a net: the primary obstacle in the tricky sport that Byron's father Don had played quite well when he represented Rhodesia in the 1950s before it became Zimbabwe.

Don reached the main draw at Wimbledon and later taught his children the game at home. All would become professionals. First came Byron, who hit two hands off both swings; then came brother Wayne and sister Cara, who did not. "I think Dad realized he made a little mistake with Byron, so he taught Wayne and I to hit with one hand off the forehand," Cara said.

Dad might have made a minor mistake, but even with less-than-optimum reach along the baseline, Don Black's very determined oldest child has become the most successful Davis Cup player in the history of his nation.

He made his debut in 1987 against Kenya in Nairobi at the age of seventeen. Zimbabwe won, but Byron would not get the chance to play his first match in the World Group until he was twenty-eight. Unlike many a World Group rookie, he would make the most of it: stunning an ailing but still able Patrick Rafter in four sets on the first day and then finishing off Jason Stoltenberg and Australia in four more sets on the third and cathartic final day.

It was a 3-2 upset for the ages, and Byron knows that the images from Mildura will keep him warm on many an early-morning bushwalk to come. He has reached the quarterfinals of the U.S. Open, been ranked number one in the world in doubles, and won the French Open with partner Jonathan Stark. But what happened in a rather remote Australian town was the exclamation point.

"I don't know what it's like to win a Grand Slam in singles, but I'll always hold this close to my heart," he said. "It was definitely the highlight of my tennis career."

It has been an atypical career, largely because of his atypical starting point. Harare might have fine weather and a refreshingly relaxed atmosphere, but it is no hub and, despite Don Black's acumen, no cutting-edge tennis laboratory.

Tennis professionals are nomads by necessity, and Byron has been more peripatetic than most. As a teenager, he attended John Newcombe's tennis academy in Texas and then went on to star at the University of Southern California. He was also a member of an ITF touring team coached by a Frenchman, Jacques Hervet, and financed by the Grand Slam Development Fund, which in turn helped the two younger Blacks. He now has an apartment in London that he often shares with Cara, but for approximately three months every year, he and his wife Fiona are able to spend time together in the place they enjoy most.

"We're so global, spending so much time all over the world, but I still can't wait to get down to Zimbabwe," he said.

It is a small pond, yet it has taken more than a decade for Byron to mature into a big fish. It was not until he and Wayne combined to upset Austria in Harare in September 1997 and then stun Australia on the road that he began consistently drawing a crowd on shopping excursions. "I think even though some of my individual achievements were reported back home, people somehow really like it when you win for your country, and they take more notice than when you play for yourself," he said.

But recognition and appreciation at home would not be Byron's only reward for toppling the Australians. He had struggled in the early spring on the hardcourts in the United States—the surface on which he has played most often in his career—but after Mildura, he suddenly recovered his balance and confidence, reaching consecutive finals in Hong Kong and Tokyo.

Davis Cup had been a launching pad for Rafter in 1997, and though it would not lift Byron to quite the same rarified heights in 1998, it certainly improved his view: "It turned my year around," Byron said.

QUARTERFINAL ROUND

Team Becker takes on team Sweden

SWEDEN d. GERMANY
Hamburg, Germany
SPAIN d. SWITZERLAND
La Coruna, Spain
ITALY d. ZIMBABWE
Prato, Italy
USA d. BELGIUM
Indianapolis, Indiana, USA
*All matches played
17–19 July, 1998*

IT WAS FRIDAY IN HAMBURG, and as Boris Becker trotted on court and on stage at the Rothenbaum Club with his familiar name rumbling through the loudspeakers and his fellow Germans roaring in appreciation, it was easy, just for a moment, to forget how much had changed.

After all, these were the introductions for a high-profile Davis Cup tie, and this was Germany hosting Sweden, the team that Becker had used as a foil in both the 1988 and 1989 Finals, when he had led his country to its first and second Davis Cup titles.

Of course, Becker had not always gotten the best of the Swedes, who defeated Germany in his first Final appearance in 1985. "There's a great rivalry here," he said.

But no matter how familiar the opponent and how loud and affirming the greeting, the semi-retired Becker was no longer the main man on court for the Germans. He would play doubles only, and though there would be rumblings and grumblings about a larger role, Becker ultimately settled for settling into his new off-court role as team manager and national tennis director, while also over-seeing the Mercedes junior team. At thirty, Becker was old for a player and young for a chief executive, but thinking small, or little of himself, has never been one of his shortcomings.

When Becker decided that 1997 would be his last year as a Grand Slam singles player, he thought hard about whether he wanted to stay involved in tennis or broaden his horizons. He chose to try and do both. "I thought about it for several months, and I realized that, as I knew tennis well and I was profoundly attached to the sport, I should try to get even more involved," he said in an interview with *L'Equipe* magazine. "I also felt that because tennis had given me so much, coaching young players would be a way for me to pay back a certain debt to the sport."

"Lots of people haven't accepted the fact that I have matured," Becker added. "They prefer to see me in tennis clothes on a court and nothing else. But I'm not seventeen anymore. I've had some good teachers in my life like Ion Tiriac and Axel Meyer-Wolden and others, and I'm a good student. I listened well and observed a lot."

But Becker's first full year as an administrator and would-be mogul was hardly without its learning experiences. For the first time since 1983, he skipped Wimbledon as a player. Instead, he went as an emissary to present a plan for a reorganized and very streamlined professional circuit in conjunction with a company called Prisma. The radical concept, which would have marginalized the ATP Tour by having top players commit to Grand Slams, Davis Cup, or Fed Cup and a few major events leading up to the Slams, was listened to carefully but ultimately rejected by the ITF, which elected not to burn its oft-repaired bridges with the ATP.

"For me, it's not really about who's winning or losing in the politics," Becker said later in the year when the ATP had succeeded in keeping its Super Nine events at least temporarily under its umbrella in the face of more Becker attempts to sway tournament directors. "Tennis has to win," Becker said, "and right now tennis is losing, and I'm trying to promote the game and bring it back to

When he was introduced to the Hamburg crowd at the opening ceremony, the roar that followed was convincing evidence that the love affair between Boris Becker and his German fans continues unabated. Summer in Indianapolis (preceding pages): The boys turn out to support the American Davis Cup team against the visitors from Belgium.

where I believe and am convinced it belongs."

For Becker, as for many others, the exclamation points need to be clearly defined in the tennis calendar: "There's too much tennis right now," he said. "It's not about the rules. It's not about best of three sets or best of five sets. It's about the sport bringing its heart and soul back on the court."

Becker brought plenty of both to a minor event the week after Wimbledon, reaching the final of the Swiss Open and beating Pioline, Felix Mantilla, and Marcelo Rios along the way. But the all-time great who has never managed to win a clay-court event would not put an end to his streak, losing to Alex Corretja in the final in straight sets.

Still, his remarkable run had Germans wondering whether Becker would play singles against the Swedes on a much quicker outdoor surface. Surprisingly, Becker did not go out of his way to end the speculation, even after he and German captain Carl-Uwe Steeb announced Tommy Haas and Nicolas Kiefer as the singles players at the draw. If Becker wanted to destabilize the Swedes, it failed: "I honestly never thought Boris would play singles," their captain, Carl-Axel Hageskog, said.

Hageskog did think Becker's renewed commitment to Davis Cup was a very positive development. "It's not only good for tennis in Germany but in the world," he said. "It's nice to see these former champions get so involved like Manuel Santana and Yannick Noah and John Newcombe. I like that. It seems like they are taking responsibility for the game. I see the same with Stefan Edberg and Anders Jarryd in our country."

Becker has delegated much responsibility to Steeb. They were teammates on the Davis Cup teams that defeated Sweden, but their friendship has a longer history than that.

"A very important part of my relationship with Charlie is that we have known each other since we were little boys," Becker said. "He doesn't have to pretend to be something he's not, and neither do I. We are really honest with each other, and if the situation is where the decision is difficult, we honestly speak about it. We don't hold back."

Hageskog and Jarryd, his assistant captain, also speak frankly, but there was less to debate than usual. The singles players would be Thomas Enqvist, who was playing arguably the best tennis of his career, and Jonas Bjorkman, who unquestionably was not.

"Jonas was struggling, but I felt in some way that I owed him the chance to play against the Germans so he could use that as a way to start playing better again," said Hageskog of Bjorkman, who comes from the same small and successful club in Vaxjo.

Bjorkman had soared to fourth in the world at the end of 1997, reaching eight finals during the season and looking impossibly fresh down the stretch. He had been the manic man of the match against the Americans, winning three rubbers, and it was his desire to plunge quickly back into the water and resume riding the wave that would ultimately cost him in 1998.

"I didn't give myself enough time to rest after Davis Cup," he said. "I felt fine, but I needed more time than I felt I needed."

Bjorkman and Magnus Larsson had resumed intense training just one week after finishing off the Americans. "We were eager to get even better for next year," said Hageskog, who coaches Larsson year-round. "They were at home in Vaxjo playing every day, running, and lifting weights. They were so pumped for the new season. It paid off a bit in the early going and then they went flat."

They also fell ill, each with a virus that proved very difficult to shake, particularly for Larsson. Bjorkman still had played well enough to win a Wimbledon warm-up in Nottingham but his ranking had dropped to nine and his confidence had headed in the same direction.

The first match of this tie would do little to change that, as Bjorkman struggled mightily with his serve, returns, and the big moments against the less experienced Haas. The Swede would get only 33 percent of his first serves in play in the opening set, which Haas finished off with an ace: his game and reversed baseball cap neatly in place.

Haas was born in Hamburg, moved to Munich, and then, at age eleven, to Nick Bollettieri's tennis academy in Bradenton, Florida. Haas's father, Peter, is a teaching professional and was convinced that Bollettieri—he of the dark shades and incandescent grin—could teach his son and daughter, Sabine, better than anyone else. Tommy and Sabine would both end up living in Bollettieri's home.

In 1997, Haas reached the semifinals of the ATP event in Hamburg, and Germans were quick to leap to conclusions: "Our New Boris" read one headline in the mass-circulation newspaper *Bild*. But while Haas is clearly a fine prospect with his big frame, increasingly effective serve, and powerful, if somewhat mechanical, one-handed groundstokes, he remains inconsistent, prone to misjudgements under pressure, and often ineffective in transition between the baseline and net.

"Tommy's game is similar to Boris's game in just about every way except coming to net," said Bollettieri, who has coached them both.

Haas is also prone to cramps in long matches, but this match—contested in front of a crowd that was often subdued despite Haas's roots—would not push either player to the limit. The best Bjorkman could do was flirt with winning the third set. He served at 5–4 and had two set points at 40–15. Haas saved the first when Bjorkman missed a forehand pass and the second when the Swede knocked another forehand long. Two points later, Haas hit a backhand pass crosscourt that Bjorkman could only lunge for and put back in play. The German ripped a short forehand at Bjorkman's body to break his serve and momentum. He then held serve and broke the Swede again to put him out of his misery, catching the last ball on the bounce and knocking it triumphantly into the stands.

"I was more confident than him, and you could see it on the big points," Haas said. "I love playing for my country, especially at home. In these moments, I always produce my best tennis."

Considering this was only Haas's second Davis Cup tie, that was quite a generalization, but there was no arguing with his Cup record of 3–0, or his emphatic 6–3, 7–6 (7–4), 7–5 victory.

Germany would not lead for long, however. Enqvist quickly and convincingly tied the tie against Kiefer with a 6–3, 6–3, 7–5 recital of controlled power and opportunism from the baseline. The fact that Kiefer had his left ankle wrapped midway through the lopsided match only encouraged the Becker singles lobby, and once again the chief executive did not exactly volunteer a vote of confidence: "I did consider playing, and I probably should have played on the last day," Becker said later. "Nicolas was emotionally very, very down, and he wasn't able to handle a big match. But I'm a player-manager now, and I have to support the young players. I don't want to knock their legs out from under them right away. First, they have to show whether they have guts or not, and Nicolas had guts. It was just that his mental state of mind was not up to par."

Kiefer, a quarterfinalist at Wimbledon in 1997 and the son of a French mother and German father, once was part of the Becker-led Mercedes team and practiced with Becker frequently. But in 1998, he decided with more than a whiff of defiance to strike out on his own, although he maintained an implicit connection by hiring Bob Brett as his coach. Brett had been Becker's coach when he won the Australian Open in 1991 and briefly became number one.

"I thought my use-by date had come up," joked Brett, who also has coached Goran Ivanisevic and Andrei Medvedev. "But it's always nice to have the challenges with these young guys."

Germany's Tommy Haas (top) and Sweden's Thomas Enqvist (bottom) were both victorious on the first day of the Germany/Sweden quarterfinal tie.

The pivotal doubles was a struggle. Hageskog thought it was one of the best in Davis Cup.

It was an outdoor tie under Friday's sunny skies (top left) but the doubles victory of Sweden's Jonas Bjorkman and Nicklas Kulti (top right) over Boris Becker and Davis Prinosil (bottom Left) was played with the roof closed (bottom right) because of heavy rain.

It was telling that Kiefer felt compelled to have Brett join him in Hamburg for the tie when there was no shortage of prospective mentors on site.

On Saturday, Becker, one of those prospective mentors, took the court with partner David Prinosil to face Bjorkman and longtime sidekick Nicklas Kulti. This pivotal match was played indoors, because rainy conditions forced the Hamburg organizers to close their stadium's new roof: more a massive umbrella than a sliding, Melbourne Park–style hatch.

Though the Germans managed to improve weather conditions on court, they unfortunately could not improve the court. Normally, the surface in the stadium in Hamburg is clay, but when Becker and Steeb wanted a hardcourt, a wood base was laid over it and a hardcourt essentially painted in layers on the wood. The result was a surface with dead spots that sent balls skidding and players' timing out of whack; it pleased neither the hosts nor the visitors.

"It was bouncing so bad that it was hard to get used to it," Bjorkman said.

The condition of the court made the high quality of play on Saturday all the more admirable. There was power and tactical expertise to spare; there was also a rare intensity. "We were so pumped up before the match because we know Becker's attitude," Bjorkman said. "Everybody knows he's great, but he still wants to show everyone that he's the best. We knew we had to go out and play aggressively and with no respect, even if he is one of the legends of tennis. If we hit him, bad luck. We had to go out with the idea of showing he was too old and mentally not let his aura get to us."

After the first set, Prinosil, Becker, and Becker's aura were in command. Kulti, visibly nervous, double-faulted twice to lose his serve and the set, but if he and Bjorkman no longer play regularly together on tour, they remain a nearly ideal cocktail of strength and quickness. It would take time and a lot of reflex volleys and clever serving, but the match would turn.

The first clue came in the second-set tiebreaker when Bjorkman hit a winning lob to give the Swedes a 5–3 lead. In the third, Kulti fired a forehand straight at Becker's head. The big German ducked, but Kulti could not avoid his glare. Yet Becker would be the one to crack in the ensuing tiebreaker, double-faulting at 5–5. On the next point, a Kulti volley struck the tape and landed short, Becker threw up a lob that was not nearly good enough to get over the explosive Bjorkman. The Swede hit an overhead straight at Becker, and the German missed.

In the fourth set, after Prinosil and Becker had broken Bjorkman to get even at 3–3, Becker proceeded to lose his serve in the next game. Bjorkman was soon performing his ungainly but somehow endearing post-victory "Brusselstep": grabbing the toe of his right sneaker with his right hand.

"One of the best Davis Cup doubles I've seen," Hageskog said with conviction.

Sweden was in command at 2–1, and in light of Enqvist's remarkable form, the semifinals seemed very much in range, but this was to be a Davis Cup season of complications for Sweden because Enqvist was no longer available. In the third set of his victory over Kiefer, he had felt something move inside his foot near the instep. It was a bone—an old soccer injury resurfacing—and when he woke up on Saturday, he could not walk without pain.

The only Swede who did not know this was Bjorkman, who was preparing to play the first reverse singles match on Sunday against the same Kiefer.

"We said nothing to Jonas because we did not want to trouble him and put more pressure on him," Hageskog said. "Jonas can handle pressure, but he was a little bit tight already. We all thought Thomas was going to win two points for us in singles, and so I think it was better that Jonas went out on court thinking that if he lost, Thomas would win."

In truth, there was far too much thinking on both sides of the court on Sunday, and the skittish surface was only part of the explanation for the skittish shotmaking from Bjorkman and Kiefer. The match, played outdoors this time in a full stadium, should have been played in private.

"We both had a big fighting heart, but it was still ugly," Bjorkman said.

Ugly and excruciatingly even, and Bjorkman did not exactly mark his territory by double-faulting to lose his serve in the opening game of the fifth set. But the Swede scrambled—it was that sort of afternoon—to break Kiefer in the ensuing game.

At 4–4, Bjorkman led 40–0 on his serve and then ended up facing two break points. He saved the first when Kiefer missed a backhand passing shot, then saved the second when Kiefer missed an even more straightforward passing shot off that same swing, which is normally his most reliable. Kiefer threw his racquet, but not just because he had missed under pressure. It was because he believed Bjorkman's second serve had been long.

With his huge calves, close-cropped hair, strong chin, and solid build, there is a pugilistic air to Kiefer: an air that the white tape wrapped around his knuckles on his playing hand during the match only accentuated. But he would not be able to fight his way out of a corner. In the next game, he fell behind 15–40 after Bjorkman successfully attacked his second serve.

He saved the first match point with a good forehand that Bjorkman lunged for and knocked into the net, but on the next point, the Swede attacked another second serve with his backhand—that stroke still worked—and Kiefer knocked a forehand passing shot into the net.

Sweden was in the semifinals, and Hageskog was soon wrapping his arms around Bjorkman and soon letting him know that Enqvist would have been in no shape to play the final rubber. "Frankly, I don't know if it was good or bad not to tell me before the match," Bjorkman said.

In fifteen Davis Cup ties, Bjorkman had now won the decisive rubber on ten occasions for Sweden. Yet somehow, in the wake of this match, he felt more relief than release: "I'm a perfectionist," he said, "and all the guys on the team are always giving me heat about how everything has to be perfect in my bag and organized in my hotel room. I'm so happy we won, but to be happy with myself, I know I have to play much better than that."

Kiefer's missed opportunity at 4–4 was difficult to digest. "That call cost me the match," he said. "It's not normal. We are in Germany. I'm sure that in Sweden, such an error would never have happened."

His comment disappointed Bjorkman: "I was surprised, because I think Nicolas is a very good guy," he said. "Unfortunately, I think you can say he doesn't have the experience being in Davis Cup. He's still very young; it's easy to make a mistake and blame it on something else instead of himself. There's a lot of pressure, because everyone thinks they are going to be as good as Becker or something."

Not even Becker was as good as Becker in Hamburg, but as Haas's victory over Larsson in the dead final rubber underscored, this rebuilding German team was still not far from building a bridge into the final four. For now, the Swedes are the leading engineers. They have reached the semifinals for seven consecutive years: no other nation compares in the 1990s. "It's so interesting to see what you can do with people when people work together," Hageskog said.

What Hageskog and the Swedes knew as they left Hamburg was that the next round might not be as tough as the first two rounds. Yes, they were playing the Spaniards and their two French Open finalists Carlos Moya and Alex Corretja, but they were playing them at home in Stockholm on the sort of indoor surface that makes sun-loving, fun-loving Spaniards long for the fresh air, eclectic architecture, and gritty courts of Barcelona.

In a match that lasted three hours, seventeen minutes and saw tremendous changes in fortune, Germany's Nicolas Kiefer (left) saved one match point but was ultimately defeated in the fifth set by Sweden's Jonas Bjorkman (opposite).

Groundstrokes instead of galleons

Manuel Santana's players had spent their quarterfinal week on clay in a less cosmopolitan corner of Spain: the Galician port of La Coruna on its western Atlantic coast. It is the same city from which the Spanish armada headed toward Great Britain and great disappointment in 1588, but La Coruna would bring better fortune to Spain's less bellicose, modern-day armada. Their opponents were the Swiss, and though Marc Rosset had once won an Olympic gold medal on clay in Spain, that was way back in 1992 before this generation of big-hitting, hard-running baseliners had come of age.

Corretja, now twenty-four, had burst to prominence before the twenty-one-year-old Moya, but as the final of Roland Garros and Moya's convincing victory had made clear, Moya was now the finest player in Spain. The 142nd-ranked Ivo Heuberger, Switzerland's number two, needed no convincing after Moya surrendered only four games in three sets in the opening rubber. Corretja was only slightly more charitable to a much better opponent, allowing Rosset five games in his straight-set victory.

Spain led 2–0 in a big hurry under the sun, and if not for Spain's now-customary struggles in the doubles on Saturday, there might have been some complaints from ticket holders about getting value for their pesetas. In their eight previous ties, the Spaniards had won only one doubles rubber: that came in 1996, when Tomas Carbonell and Corretja defeated Denmark to help lift Spain out of Group One and into the World Group. Part of the problem has been continuity, yet Santana elected to use Spain's ninth different combination in its last nine doubles rubbers. This time it would be veteran Javier Sanchez and huge-serving Davis Cup rookie Julian Alonso, who had a stronger Swiss connection than any of his teammates (he was dating world number one Martina Hingis).

Hingis diplomatically stayed away from La Coruna, but the Spanish press was less diplomatic about the new pairing. Doubles remains our "talon de Aquiles," wrote one reporter. Sanchez and Alonso would do better than some of their predecessors, pushing the busy Rosset and partner Lorenzo Manta to five sets, but when push came to shove, the Swiss closed the gap to 2–1 with a 3–6, 6–3, 6–4, 5–7, 6–2 victory that required slightly more than three hours.

Considering that doubles has a lot to do with camaraderie and communication, it is surprising that the Spaniards, with their bonhomie and tight bonds, cannot field a stronger pair. "Our best boys just don't play doubles," Santana said. "So I'm going to go with this team for a while. I think it's the best I can do at the moment."

The good news was that there would be meaningful tennis on Sunday, but Moya quickly extinguished the suspense by beating Rosset in straight sets to put Spain in the semifinals for the first time since 1987.

It had been a rough weekend in singles for Rosset, but his luck would not be all bad in 1998. Less than two months later, after losing early in the U.S. Open, he booked seats on a Swissair flight for Geneva with his coach Pierre Simsolo. Rosset then changed his mind the afternoon of the flight and decided to stay in New York to train for at least one more day. That night, a friend called Rosset in his hotel and told him to turn on the television. The flight crashed into the Atlantic Ocean, killing all 229 passengers aboard. Another member of the tennis community, Pierre Babolat, was not as forunate. The head of the string manufacturing company, Babolat was among those who died in the crash.

"Really, I should have been on this plane, so I am so happy to have a chance to still be alive," Rosset would say in New York. "But I am also very sad for the victims and the families. They showed footage of the families waiting at the airport in Geneva. It just makes your heart hurt."

The mighty Spaniards—captain Manual Santana, Carlos Moya, Julien Alonso, Alex Corretja, and Javier Sanchez (opposite, top)— reached their first semifinal round in more than twenty years after Moya (opposite, bottom) and Corretja (top) turned in solid victories over the Swiss team, led by Marc Rosset (bottom).

The Zimbabweans' turn to roast

By the time Moya defeated Rosset, the other two semifinalists already had begun celebrating. In Prato, near Florence, on Saturday, the Italians had taken a 3–0 lead after the doubles, giving Zimbabwe no hope of a renaissance on Tuscan clay. On the same day, in the considerably less evocative community of Indianapolis, the Americans, still without Sampras, had a 3–0 lead over the Belgians.

After a first round that had been one of the more compelling in memory, the quarterfinals had produced one stirring encounter and three from which it was often necessary to stir. But the over-achieving Italians, somehow in their third consecutive semifinal, were not complaining about the absence of drama, and to be honest, neither were the Black brothers. By beating Australia, they already had made their Davis Cup campaign a success, and in Prato, their spirited but ineffectual play merely confirmed that the courts at their family fief in Zimbabwe were made of grass, not clay.

The brothers were still big in Harare, however, and Byron had finally gotten his domestic ovation for the Australian upset when he had returned home two weeks later (by that time, Zimbabwean television had finally broadcast the tie at home). "Not quite as big a greeting as Wayne's of course," Byron said. "I had dances and a few ministers from the government and close friends and family to welcome me. You don't get that experience too often, and you've got to cherish when it happens. You know, Sampras and some other guys moan about Davis Cup. They think it's too much for their schedules. Coming from a small country like Zimbabwe, Wayne and I get to play every time, and we love the honor. We don't get paid a lot. There are other things we could be doing to make more money, but we will always stick it in our schedule."

The Italians also have no problem finding room in their calendars, and by July, they were clearly no longer as weak a team as they had appeared in the early going. Number one Andrea Gaudenzi had enjoyed a respectable clay-court season, and new number two Davide Sanguinetti had enjoyed a better-than-respectable Wimbledon, capitalizing on a clement draw to become the first Italian to reach the quarterfinals since Adriano Panatta in 1979.

At twenty-five, Sanguinetti was a much later bloomer than Panatta (the flecks of gray in his hair only accentuated it), but after spending most of the previous five seasons on the satellite and Challenger circuits, he would leave Prato as a Davis Cup mainstay and a popular public figure. After Gaudenzi beat Wayne Black in the opening rubber 6–3, 6–3, 6–4, Sanguinetti was even more dominant against Byron, winning 6–3, 6–3, 6–0 and smacking deep, forceful shots consistently and rushing the net selectively and effectively. "When it ended, I felt as good as at Wimbledon," Sanguinetti said. "I felt like God was remote-controlling me out there or something."

Gaudenzi and Diego Nargiso were not quite as ethereal on Saturday but still defeated the Blacks in four sets on Saturday to win a trip to the United States in September. The only thing the Italians got wrong was their destination. They were convinced they were heading for San Diego (it made several headlines, too). As it turned out, they were all heading for the less sunlit city of Milwaukee, and they would not be the only players to express disappointment at that choice.

Andre Agassi would also find fault with it, but when the United States played Belgium in another midwestern city in the quarterfinals, Agassi was back in the lineup, and he had company. For the first time since captain Tom Gullikson assumed his post in 1994, he selected the same four-man team in consecutive ties. Gullikson does not thrive on change: his ever-shifting lineup has merely been a testimony to the difficulty he has had getting top players to commit consistently.

Zimbabwean fans (top) have a lot to celebrate as their Davis Cup team (bottom) played in the elite World Group for the first time in 1998. From left: Byron Black, Genius Chidzikwe, Captain Gavin Siney, Rashid Hassan, Wayne Black.

The Italians, perennial overachievers, were in their third consecutive semifinal.

Italy's Andrea Gaudenzi (top left) and Davide Sanguinetti (top middle) gave Italy a 2–0 start over Zimbabwe. The Italian fans (top right) cheered doubles partners Diego Nargiso and Gaudenzi (bottom left) on to victory. The win secured a place for Captain Paolo Bertolucci's team (bottom right) in the semifinals.

A Renaissance man from Vegas

When 1997 was drawing to a close, Agassi was no longer a top player. His ranking had dropped to 141, as low as it had been since he was sixteen and in his first year on tour. Coach Brad Gilbert was close to looking for work elsewhere, but Agassi decided to rebuild a foundation, playing in two Challenger events in the United States and winning one of them. "Once I decided to get back to work, I knew I had to start at the level I was at, and that level was the Challenger level," Agassi said.

By the time he agreed to face the Belgians, he was back in the top 20, although he had not made it past the first round at the French Open or the second round at Wimbledon. "It's definitely something I need right now," Agassi said of the Davis Cup quarterfinal.

After Jim Courier had defeated Belgium's number one, Filip Dewulf, in four sets, Agassi took apart Belgium's first-round savior, Christophe Van Garsse, 6–2, 6–2, 6–2. Van Garsse was visibly overwhelmed by the occasion, and when he shook Agassi's hand after the match, he thanked him for the honor and continued to give him more compliments than he had problems from the baseline.

"I saw him playing on television so many times," said Van Garsse, offering a clue to some of his difficulties. "I couldn't imagine that somebody could play so fast on the ball and put so much pressure on me. I could be disappointed, but I'm twenty-four, and I'm not a super talent. I'm a good player. I can beat a lot of good players, but I'm realistic."

It was a tie and a round for realists. The only hint of fantasy in the midst of the shimmering Indianapolis heat came from an eighteen-year-old Belgian with a huge forehand who calls himself X-man and has taken a shine to the ever-evolving (devolving?) moods and hair hues of American basketball player Dennis Rodman. Xavier Malisse stuck with peroxide blond locks in Indianapolis, but he has opted for bright red and avocado green in the past. He had nearly stunned Sampras in an indoor event in February, and his spirited play in his Davis Cup debut alongside Johan van Herck made Saturday's doubles a great deal more compelling than Friday's singles. Courier and Todd Martin would ultimately prevail in five sets.

"I think if all eighteen-year-olds had his type of talent, it would be pretty scary," said Martin, after beating Malisse in straight sets in the first of Sunday's reverse singles matches. "But you know there needs to be temperance. It's a matter of choosing the right shots and realizing that although he can hit winners from five feet behind the baseline, it's not necessarily the proper play. He'll learn."

Though Sunday's matches were meaningless, the day was not without meaningful gestures. Before play began, a ceremony was held in remembrance of Todd Witsken, the former professional player and director of the Indianapolis Tennis Center. Witsken had died of brain cancer at age thirty-four in May, leaving his wife to raise four children under the age of seven. As part of their compensation for playing Davis Cup, the Americans receive $25,000 each round to donate to the charity of their choice. This time, all four team members chose to donate their share to the Witsken family, and the United States Tennis Association and local organizing committee brought the total to $115,000.

It was money well and generously spent, although there was still plenty to go around in the American locker room. Singles players on the American team in 1998 received $100,000 each per round; doubles players, $50,000. It had still not been enough to lure Sampras or Chang to Indianapolis in July, but then the Americans had not needed Sampras or Chang.

The situation would be quite different in Milwaukee in September.

The U.S. team of Todd Martin (top) and Jim Courier won the decisive match, defeating Belgian teen sensation Xavier Malisse (bottom) and Johan van Herck in five tightly fought sets. Opposite: On opening day, the USA's Andre Agassi (top left) defeated Christophe Van Garsse (top right) while Belgian Filip Dewulf (bottom left) fell to Jim Courier (bottom right).

Jim Courier

"THAT'S KIND OF WHAT IT'S ALL ABOUT FOR ME, creating the memories," said Jim Courier on the eve of the Davis Cup quarterfinals.

Courier was once the world's top-ranked player: a strapping, super-fit portrait of backhand-avoiding, pace-seeking focus from the baseline. He won two Australian Opens, two French Opens and reached the finals of the two other Grand Slam events. But such success is now firmly part of the past for the American with the baseball cap yanked low and the intensity cranked high.

At age twenty-seven, he is still a draw: still a meaty interview and an intriguing blend of roughcut bristle and self-improving curiosity. But the number next to his name every week no longer matches his resume. He was ranked 47th when he took the court against Belgium's Filip Dewulf in Indianapolis, and his last Grand Slam final was Wimbledon in 1993.

It has been a question of health: he has suffered injuries to his knee, shoulder, and, most recently, his playing arm. It has also been a question of evolution: "When Jim won his French Opens, he was hitting the ball harder under control than anyone else out there," said Courier's former coach Jose Higueras. "That is not the way it is anymore."

Courier never relished being a lightning rod for public attention. "I always, always have said that I'd rather be rich than famous," he once observed. But he remains a proud and ambitious fellow, and he has found meaning and a measure of solace in an event that has a relatively low profile in the United States and a relatively high profile elsewhere. "The Davis Cup and the Grand Slams are the two reasons I get up every morning and strap on my shoes and go practice," he said in Indianapolis.

"For anyone who has played as long as Jim, a first-round match on tour gets a little mundane, but Davis Cup gets his juices flowing," said American captain Tom Gullikson. "You don't have to wade through three or four opponents to get to a meaningful match."

Courier was born and raised in Florida, but unlike some other racquet-wielding denizens of his state, he has seldom been a sunshine patriot. He has declined to play Davis Cup in the past, skipping the 1993 first-round loss in Australia and the 1996 quarterfinal loss in the Czech Republic. But he has played on two winning teams, and in the last two seasons, has made himself available consistently, even if that meant observing from the bench as a reserve, as he did at the 1997 semifinals in Washington D.C. against the Australians.

Courier did not have much time to observe in Indianapolis. After beating Dewulf on Friday, he was drafted to play doubles with Martin on Saturday because of a knee injury to Richey Reneberg. He and Martin had played doubles together in a tournament only once, and that was in 1995. But experience would make the difference, and Courier would improve his nation's record in ties in which he has played to 12–0. "You don't talk about a no-hitter when you're in the dugout," he said, making good use of a baseball analogy.

There was a time when Courier preferred baseball to tennis, and perhaps it is fitting that the "dead arm" that has troubled him the last two seasons—tightness and a loss of strength—is the sort of condition pitchers sometimes develop. Courier blames some of it on his technique: "I don't think the human arm was designed to do what I asked mine to do." He blames some of it on the recent trend on tour and at Wimbledon to opt for heavier balls. "They're hurting a lot of guys, and I'm one of them," Courier said.

The pain would keep Courier from winning his third match of the tie, as he chose to withdraw against Van Garsse in the final reverse singles. It was a rubber that was as dead as Courier's arm, yet it was still another in a lengthening string of nasty omens for Courier's future in the sport he once dominated. "I'm afraid Jim is really nearing the end of his rope, and I'm very sorry about it," said United States Tennis Association president Harry Marmion. "He's a hell of a warrior."

No longer a major threat to win majors, the warrior was still a threat in another best-of-five set forum in Indianapolis. Beating Belgians isn't quite like beating Spaniards or Swedes, but it puts yet another memory in the bank of the man who is chasing them in what bears a very strong resemblance to the twilight.

An American
lakeside retreat.

SWEDEN d. SPAIN
Stockholm, Sweden
ITALY d. USA
Milwaukee, Wisconsin, USA
*Matches played
25–27 September, 1998*

THERE WERE THE CUTTING, CLEVER WORDS FROM ANDRE AGASSI at the U.S. Open. There were the unsold tickets at the box office; the wrong surface and the wrong team, which played—with all due respect to the pleasant and prosperous city of Milwaukee—in the wrong place.

The Americans might have had the homecourt advantage over the Italians in their Davis Cup semifinal, but by the time the matches actually began, the hosts had done a remarkably exhaustive job of eliminating that psychological edge.

"We still have a good chance, but it seems like it is getting to be less and less, and whenever that momentum changes, it is hard to stop," said Agassi presciently several weeks before the tie.

Agassi, of course, was one of those responsible for the momentum shift. He did not play, but if his former, and not necessarily future, teammates had kept their wits and groundstrokes in play during tiebreakers, they could still, even without him or Pete Sampras or Michael Chang, have put the United States in the Final for the second consecutive year. But the Italians, who brought their best players and attitude to the shores of Lake Michigan, were not carrying nearly as much emotional baggage as the nation that created the Cup in 1900 and has won it a record thirty-one times.

It would not be fair to say that the team that wanted it more turned out to be the winner in Milwaukee. Anyone who has seen Todd Martin go misty over his flag or Justin Gimelstob wave one energetically in the stands knows that the Americans who did care to compete cared a great deal. But it would be very fair to say that the team whose nation and tennis community wanted it more turned out to be the winner.

"Italians don't follow us much when we play on the tour," Gaudenzi would say. "But when it gets to Davis Cup, when there is a flag involved, Italy is very emotional."

An overachiever generally generates more emotion than an underachiever, and the Italians, with no players ranked in the top 35 were even more unlikely finalists than the French in 1996, when the French won the Cup by upsetting the Swedes in a tie with more twists and turns than the Stockholm coastline. The French at least had Cedric Pioline, who had reached the final at the U.S. Open and would later do the same at Wimbledon.

What these Italians had was Andrea Gaudenzi, a gifted but injury-prone player who had never gotten further than the fourth round at a Slam, and Davide Sanguinetti, who was having a breakthrough year at the relatively advanced age of twenty-five but was still only 47th in the world. The Italians also had Diego Nargiso, a good but not extremely good doubles player whose left-handed returns and volleys are often flashy but not always foolproof.

What the Americans had was not much more imposing, and to understand why it is important to retreat from Milwaukee for a moment and turn back the clock to late November 1997, when Sampras was sitting on a couch in a luxury hotel suite in Gothenburg, Sweden, with his leg elevated and his mood heading in the opposite direction. He had come reluctantly to the Final against the

Swedes. Number one in the world for the fifth consecutive year, he was satisfied, he was sated, and he wanted a break much more than another working week. He would soon get that break but only at the price of injury: tearing his calf slightly in the second singles rubber of the Final against Magnus Larsson. "The season is just too long," Sampras said, almost angrily.

The Americans were on their way to a 5–0 defeat, and captain Tom Gullikson was already doing his best to spin the focus ahead as he expressed his hopes and fears in the corridors of the Scandinavium in Gothenburg. How will this affect the team? he was asked.

"You'd have to ask the players, but if I was a player, I'd want to play even more next year to help us win," he said. "If we feel we have the best players, the only way to prove it is to win this. Losing in the Final only makes me hungrier."

But Sampras would elect to fast in 1998. "*Less is more* is my philosophy with Davis Cup," said Sampras, who, nonetheless, had no problem with quantity when he chose to play six straight European indoor tournaments in the fall in a successful attempt to keep his number-one ranking.

"I talked to Pete quite a bit, and his heart just was not into playing Davis Cup, and it's hard to change what's in someone's heart," Gullikson said. "I tried to use my persuasiveness and logic, but if this thing was in his heart, he should be asking me to play and not the other way around."

Agassi required no convincing when the season began, but there would be a proviso. He had a scheduling conflict during the semifinals because he had organized a charity event for his foundation in Las Vegas on the same weekend in late September.

"We get the arena certain days and get the talent on certain days, and that is the only way it is going to happen," Agassi said of the event.

Gullikson and USTA officials were well aware of this, because Agassi's agent Perry Rogers informed them of the conflict shortly after the year began. "Perry told me that Andre will help you out the first couple of rounds and probably won't be available the week of the semis," Gullikson said. "My thinking the whole year was that he wouldn't be available."

Then in July, as the United States and Agassi were making quick, if sweaty, work of Belgium in steamy Indianapolis in the quarterfinals, Agassi revised the plan and informed Gullikson that he would be willing to play if the United States Tennis Association could find a semifinal site in the West. He would spend the week with the team, play singles on Friday, then fly to his charity event on Saturday and be back in time to play some more for his country on Sunday.

For Agassi, San Diego, which had expressed lukewarm interest in hosting the semifinal, was a good choice, and his hometown Las Vegas was the perfect choice.

"I mean we could easily have played in Vegas," he said after the fact. "Give me three phone calls; I will get it done."

But it was not up to Agassi, which, according to the young man who wants more player control, was a bug in the system, and the USTA and its representatives did not get it done. According to Gullikson, negotiations already were well underway with prospective host cities before Agassi told him he wanted to play, which made it difficult to reverse course. But there was more to it than that.

Privately, there was resistance from some of Agassi's teammates at the idea of him treating the semifinal like a runway: touching down and taking off as he pleased. "Those were the vibrations we got from the players," said USTA president Harry Marmion. "Andre does Davis Cup his own way. He never plays a dead rubber. When the tie is over in Indianapolis and we've got our three points, everybody hangs around, but Andre gets the cell phone and says to the plane, 'Come get me.' Andre takes

In only his fourth tie as captain, Paolo Bertolucci (top) led the Italian team to its first Davis Cup Final since 1980 by virtue of a semifinal victory over team USA, led by Tom Gullikson (bottom). Preceding pages: Sweden's Jonas Bjorkman, shown here after his victory over Spain's Carlos Moya, always wears his feelings very close to the surface.

off, and we never see him again."

There was also the television issue—the nine-hour time difference between the West Coast and continental Europe is bad for European broadcasters—and the financial issue: Milwaukee with its newly refurbished arena was offering $250,000 for the right to host the tie with or without Agassi. That was considerably more than any other city, including San Diego or Las Vegas, was willing to pay in a country where Davis Cup is no main event, particularly in September with Major League Baseball and the National Football League dominating the small screen.

According to Gullikson, the fact that he grew up in Wisconsin had nothing to do with Milwaukee's selection. "I certainly didn't lobby for it," Gullikson said. "My wife Julie's comment was, 'All that means is there are going to be five hundred people who beat you in the juniors who remember you and who all want tickets.'"

No love games

It was a typically self-deprecating comment from Gullikson, and it came after Agassi was plenty deprecating of him and the USTA during a post-match news conference at Flushing Meadows.

Agassi on the choice of site: "It never ceases to amaze me what decisions get made without the players' input."

Agassi on the USTA's choice of Gullikson as captain: "I think there is probably a lot of fear factor giving up the reins. That is why John McEnroe didn't get the job. Here is someone who has done as much for Davis Cup as anybody, and he didn't get the job because he is going to speak his mind. They'd rather have somebody down there where they know they can pull some strings, and they definitely have that."

Agassi on whether he would play the Final if the U.S. beat Italy without him: "If it was in my backyard, I wouldn't walk out the back door."

The next day, Gullikson found Agassi in the U.S. Open locker room and attempted to set the record straight. "We had a good chat for about twenty minutes," Gullikson said. "I basically told him that he had meant a lot to Davis Cup over the years and obviously it had meant a lot to him. And I suggested that he try to speak about it a bit more positively. He does care about Davis Cup, and obviously he was frustrated and venting a bit, and when Andre vents the whole world hears about it."

The steam had yet to clear, however. The following day at Flushing Meadows, Justin Gimelstob's father, Barry, confronted Agassi's coach Brad Gilbert and accused him of trying to position himself to take over Gullikson's job by influencing Agassi to be critical. The two nearly came to blows, and Barry Gimelstob also said Gilbert had been rude to his son in the locker room at the event in Los Angeles earlier in the year. Gilbert told *Tennis* magazine that Gimelstob's accusations were "crazy stuff," suggesting that Barry was angry because Andre had downplayed Justin's star potential and that Gimelstob was "just stressed out about tennis, like a lot of other tennis fathers."

It was a new low-water mark for the divided and soon-to-be-conquered American camp, and it certainly did not help the Davis Cup brain trust's collective mood when Agassi ripped through Sanguinetti, 6–2, 6–3, 6–0, in the second round the next day and then added another one-liner to his large body of work at the Open. Asked what he would do if he were president of the USTA, Agassi responded, "I wouldn't have anybody who wears a tie make a decision."

He would have more to say about the USTA president later, but the more important question was whether the USTA's choice of the most financially attractive site was really good business. Considering the way Sampras feels about Davis Cup, was it wise to risk alienating the American superstar who does care about it for a $250,000 guarantee? If the Davis Cup were in a position of domestic strength, the USTA's reasoning would have been more difficult to question. But as that is not the case, why not cater to Agassi, one of the most prominent athletes in the United States?

"You have to be pathetic to take the best U.S. Davis Cup player and absolutely make him never want to play again," Agassi said after the tie.

"I guess what we should have done is go back to Andre much earlier in the year and see if we could make it possible," said Gullikson, who regrets that Milwaukee was announced as the site before he could talk to Agassi directly.

"I took a family vacation after Indianapolis," Gullikson said. "I didn't follow up as quickly as I could have. That was my miscommunication."

The American team did have one gate attraction on its team in Milwaukee: Jim Courier. "Frankly I think it's a shame the way it's gone down with Andre: the way he's been talking," Courier said. After skipping the U.S. Open because of his chronically sore arm and mulling his future, Courier telephoned Gullikson and said he wanted to be part of the effort. The captain agreed but told Courier that in light of his lack of recent matchplay, he was not guaranteed to be in the lineup.

The other members of the team would be Martin and two twenty-one-year-old Davis Cup rookies, Jan-Michael Gambill and Gimelstob, who both had served as practice partners and cheerleaders in previous ties but had yet to step between the lines.

The day the team gathered on site, Gullikson, Martin, and Gimelstob attended a Milwaukee Brewers/St. Louis Cardinals baseball game. The biggest sports story of the summer in the United States had been Mark McGwire's pursuit of Babe Ruth's single-season home-run record. The Cardinals' first baseman had broken it during the U.S. Open, and after Gullikson had thrown out the ceremonial first pitch and missed the strike zone (omen-trackers, take note), McGwire presently slammed his sixty-fifth homer of the year. As his blast cleared the wall, the late-arriving Courier was walking in a tunnel toward the ballpark. It would hardly be the only action he would miss in Milwaukee.

The next evening, as the team drove to a nearby airport for an ad hoc photo op with United States Vice President Al Gore, Courier missed the hand-shaking because he got back late from the gym (or because he was a Republican). The extra workout time did not help his practice performance, and when Gullikson announced his team at the draw, Courier's name was not on the list. It would be Martin and Gambill in singles; Martin and Gimelstob in doubles, which was no great surprise and no great compliment to the current state of Courier's game. "I didn't come here thinking I wouldn't play, but once I was here I kind of got the feeling that that was the way Gully was leaning," Courier told the *New York Times*. "As it turns out, I guess I'm the ace on the bench."

"If Jim would have been beating everyone 6–1 in practice it certainly might have been different," Gullikson said.

It was still a risky move, considering Gambill's dearth of big-match experience and Courier's wealth of it. But Gullikson felt that the moment was propitious to give Gambill his chance. He was quite confident that Martin could win both his singles matches indoors and that the Americans, even with the rookie factor, could win another point somewhere else.

The trouble was, the Italians were also feeling rather confident, and not simply because the main American men were all missing, but because the hardcourt that their hosts had laid down was

"Hollywood" may have had the star power but Gaudenzi had the edge in experience.

Named after a TV actor and blessed with star-quality good looks, Jan-Michael Gambill (above, left and right) made his Davis Cup debut for the United States against Italy but lost the opening singles to the wily veteran Andrea Gaudenzi (right).

to their liking. It was relatively slow and relatively suited to their baseline, counter-punching games.

"When we practiced in Italy, we practiced on a really fast surface, and when we came here we were a little surprised," said team member Gianluca Pozzi. The Italians were not alone. Gullikson said he had ordered a medium-speed court with a high bounce. What he said he got was a slow court with a low bounce. In 1996, when the United States defeated the Spaniards in the Fed Cup final in Atlantic City, New Jersey, the USTA's Fed Cup chairman Carole Graebner did not like the indoor court that had been laid down before play began and ordered it changed. The Spaniards, who already had practiced on the first court, were understandably displeased; the Americans were fined but the new court had its desired effect. It might have been worth risking another fine in Milwaukee, but this time there would be no hammering and gluing into the night.

"Tom thought it was a little bit slow but he didn't feel that was going to be the issue," Marmion said. "It turned out to be a big issue. Even as an amateur, I could tell the volleys had no bite to them. The Italians were able to return a lot of balls that on a faster court they would not have been able to return. We had the wrong court, and I think that's Tom's responsibility, and I think he knows that, and I don't think it will ever happen again."

Friends, Romans, fortunate men

It had been a season of pleasant surprises for the Italian team. The year before, they had reached the semifinals with Renzo Furlan and Omar Camporese playing singles, but both players' form had slipped: Furlan's partly because of an injury to his playing hand. The only on-court links to that 1997 team were Nargiso and captain Paolo Bertolucci, who had taken over before the semifinal loss in Sweden when his longtime doubles partner Adriano Panatta had angrily resigned because of a conflict with the Italian Tennis Federation. Bertolucci and Panatta had both played Davis Cup against the Americans in the 1979 Final: a Final the Americans won, 5–0. But then, Americans usually did win against Italians. In nine previous ties, the Italians had prevailed only twice: in 1960 and 1961 when Nicola Pietrangeli was their leading clay-court master and toastmaster.

Pietrangeli was in Milwaukee, and what he saw on the opening day must have made him very nostalgic, except for the several thousand empty seats inside the Milwaukee Arena. Gambill faced Gaudenzi in the opening rubber, and though Gaudenzi had needed a cortisone shot to deaden the pain in the fragile right shoulder that he had reinjured at the U.S. Open, he at least had been around long enough to be immunized against Davis Cup jitters. Gambill was in disturbingly new, if not enemy, territory and played like it in the first set, losing 6–2. "I don't think I've ever been that nervous," he said later. "But it went away after the first set."

Which partly explains how he managed to win the second, 6–0, dominating with his serve, quick feet, and two-handed groundstrokes. Gambill had already shown the potential to be a factor on tour in 1998, having leaped from a ranking of 227 in January to 50 in September.

"Last year I was struggling to get into tournaments, and now I'm representing my country," Gambill said with a certain amount of wonder.

Nicknamed "Hollywood" by his teammates because of his blond, good looks and affluent background (he didn't have to wait to reach the top 10 to drive a Jaguar), Gambill actually came from a place farther north: Spokane, Washington. It is a rainy place, and Gambill played plenty of indoor tennis as he learned the game. But against Gaudenzi, he never quite learned to handle the moment in front of a crowd of that was announced at 6,071.

"Which just goes to show that tennis fans spend a lot of time on the concourse or they're extremely thin," wrote Dale Hofmann, a columnist for the *Milwaukee Journal Sentinel*.

However many witnesses there were, they did not begin to give full voice to their jingoism until after Gambill had lost the third set in a tiebreaker, 7–0. It was an oddly decisive setback considering that Gambill had rallied from a 2–5, two-break deficit to force the tiebreaker. The best thing Gambill did in the next set was save eight match points on his serve, which was enough to cause Gaudenzi to receive a point penalty for breaking his second racquet of the match but not enough to extend Gambill's painfully public learning experience.

When he missed his final short forehand of the match to lose the tiebreaker 7–4, he walked toward the net with a slightly vacant expression. He did not look much better after he slumped in his chair courtside, barely looking up as Bertolucci ambled over and grabbed his hand.

"The first match in Davis Cup is very, very difficult for anybody," Gaudenzi said graciously. "I just think that in both tiebreaks, I always tried to play more aggressive than him."

Martin would prove the more aggressive player against Sanguinetti, but it would not improve the Americans' bottom line. For Gullikson, a sense of dread began to build early in the match when he saw that Martin's normally incisive approach shots and groundstrokes were not penetrating effectively on the slow surface. Like Gambill, Martin had grown up playing indoor tennis in his often snowbound home state of Michigan, but this was no typical indoor court.

"I'm not big on excuses, but that was close to the slowest court I played on all year," Martin would say later. Early in the match, Sanguinetti trailed 15–30 on his serve and hit a second serve (not his strength) that Martin attacked and followed to net. Sanguinetti's next shot should have given Martin a shoulder-high backhand volley, but the big American let the ball go, and it landed about a foot inside the court. "That sent me a message that Todd was a little tight," Gullikson said.

When Sanguinetti won the first-set tiebreaker 7–0, the message was very clear, and the very fleet Sanguinetti was soon gathering speed: passing, returning, and retrieving with great confidence in a country where he once played collegiately for UCLA but never nearly as well as this. The Italian would win the final two sets by the scores of 6–3 and 7–6 (10–8) and make a lot of new friends at home in the process. "Todd was the favorite, but I think in Davis Cup we can see that nobody is the favorite," he said.

Perhaps not, but the Italians were definitely and deservedly favorites now, and their doubles team of Gaudenzi and Nargiso had a lot more experience in Davis Cup than Martin and Gimelstob, whom Gullikson declined to replace with Courier.

"I don't like to second guess myself; you can do that," Gullikson told reporters. Later he would be more expansive: "Justin had been playing really well in practice; it was time for him to play, and the only way you're going to get experience is to be thrown out there: even 2–0 down," Gullikson explained. What Gimelstob had in his corner was his vitality. During the team's first practice on Monday, he was ripping shots, shouting, "USA, USA, USA," and doing his own running commentary: "And somebody from the crowd yells, 'Go Gimel!'"

There was nothing unusual about this. "He has so much energy and enthusiasm, which is not the first thing you would say about me," the more reflective Martin observed. "I've got the calm, cool, collected side, which is certainly not the first thing you would say about him. The more off the record his jokes should be the more he wants them on the record."

Playing in the United States was no new thing for former UCLA star Davide Sanguinetti of Italy (top), who handily defeated American Todd Martin (bottom) in the second singles.

In the court of King Gustav

By the time the doubles teams walked on court on Saturday in Milwaukee, it was already public knowledge that Sweden was in the Final. They got there by dismissing the Spaniards with relative ease in Stockholm on an indoor carpet that was as quick as indoor carpets are supposed to be when laid with the intention of giving attacking players an edge. The Spaniards would certainly have preferred the medium-speed hardcourt that was lying underneath: Alex Corretja and Carlos Moya would stunningly reach the final of the ATP Tour Championships indoors on a similar surface in November.

While the Americans had typically dreamed big and ended up with too few tickets sold, the Swedes had typically planned conservatively and ended up with a sellout. With its narrow, well-worn wooden bleachers, the Kungliga Tennishallen is no modern sports palace. It is a cramped, atmospheric place with a mere four thousand seats and a past. Constructed during World War II while Sweden was busy staying neutral, it was the first indoor arena built expressly for the sport that Sweden's King Gustav V enjoyed above all others. And it was in this same "Royal Tennis Hall" in 1975 that Bjorn Borg clinched Sweden's first Davis Cup title and celebrated by leaping over the net.

It was the start of something remarkable, and Borg was in the stands for the first night of these semifinals as the Swedes attempted to put another brick on the Davis Cup edifice for which he laid the foundation. Over the years, Borg has seldom expressed interest in watching others play the game he mastered, but he had good reason for breaking the habit: his son Robin was a ballboy for this tie.

Though Borg's life had changed considerably since 1975, some areas of the Kungliga appeared not to have changed for longer than that. Yes, there were now titanium racquets and very expensive tennis shoes (even for Sweden) in the small pro shop, but a bookcase in a reading room upstairs was filled with treatises on tennis not by Bollettieri, Braden, or even Borg, but by Bill Tilden, Suzanne Lenglen, Rene Lacoste, and Budge Patty. There were also numerous black-and-white photos of King Gustav, also known as "Mr. G," in his long-sleeved, all-white tennis garb, looking as gaunt as a Giacometti sculpture.

It had been fifteen years since the Swedish capital had hosted a Davis Cup tie: a remarkable gap that is a reflection of tennis's waning popularity in the last decade in this nation of 8.8 million that has produced a disproportionate number of fine players. But the dramatic 1996 Final loss to France in Malmo and the crushing defeat of Sampras and the Americans in the 1997 Final in Gothenburg had begun to change the momentum.

Jonas Bjorkman, with his open manner and fine comedic timing, had become a relatively popular figure at home. There was renewed interest from youngsters in taking lessons and a leap in Swedish Tennis Association membership from approximately 110,000 to 125,000 (it was near 190,000 when Borg was at his peak). There was also a new contract with Swedish public television, which didn't even broadcast the 1996 Final but was planning coverage of the semifinal this year.

"I think the Final last year was a turning point," said Jan Francke, the STA president. Francke would have preferred a bigger arena than the Kunglighalle, but it was either four thousand seats there or fifteen thousand in the Globe Arena, and the Globe was considered too big and expensive by Swedish tennis officials, who have occasionally been criticized by the players for their languid promotion of Davis Cup ties. "There are no intermediate options in Stockholm," Francke said.

So nostalgia it would be, and not just for the Swedes. Spanish captain Manuel Santana had played Davis Cup outdoors on clay at the Kunglighalle in a second round zonal match in 1960.

Both Sweden and Spain enjoyed their supporters at the semifinal round in Stockholm. Although the host country (top) naturally enjoyed the larger number, the visitor's fans (bottom) were both noisy and colorful.

Santana had lost both his singles rubbers and the Swedes had won 3–2. Santana later took his revenge on Spanish clay in 1968, and his Stockholm experience certainly did not sour him on the country. He later married a Swede and regularly visits his in-laws in Gothenburg.

"It's a special tie for me," Santana said. "And I think both these teams are very similar. It seems like they are all good friends with each other, and it seems that both teams are very eager to play Davis Cup. I know the Swedes only play for the prize money, just like we do. There are no appearance fees or guarantees."

Santana's singles players, Carlos Moya and Alex Corretja, were comfortably positioned in the top 10. Moya had reached the semifinals of the U.S. Open, defeating Corretja in straight sets in the fourth round. He already had beaten him in the final of the French Open in June, but their friendship was clearly intact. All one had to do was watch them communicate freely and easily during practice.

"They are millionaires but such nice boys," Santana said. "They don't have huge heads. I don't know how long I will be with them but as long as I'm with them I'm happy. I'm getting younger, not older."

When Moya was eleven, he asked his mother, Pilar, if she would take a picture of him with the older Corretja, who was then dominating the Spanish junior events. But they would not truly meet until much later, when Juan Avendano, the former Spanish Davis Cup captain, asked Corretja if he would hit with a young and very promising seventeen-year-old who had recently moved from the Balearic island of Mallorca to Barcelona to train. It was Moya, and what Corretja remembers most from their encounter was what happened when he asked Moya to come to net and hit some volleys. "He was so shy, and he refused because he said he didn't volley well at all," Corretja said.

Volleying remains a Spanish weakness, and it is not simply a question of technique, although Corretja's is less than ideal. It also a question of confidence and of sensing when to push forward from the baseline. Neither Spanish star would sense it nearly often enough on the first day when Corretja faced Bjorkman and Moya faced Thomas Johansson on the Taraflex surface. Corretja had practiced on the same surface in Barcelona before arriving in Sweden, but with only one permanent indoor court, the Catalan capital is hardly the place to improve one's ability to succeed under a roof.

"We need to build more indoor courts," Corretja said. "Our federation is making an effort, but it would really help our tennis and the young guys coming up." Playing against Bjorkman, he never served and volleyed in the match and rarely came to net at all. If one used the computer as a guideline, the outcome was a mild surprise. Bjorkman was ranked 13th in the world; Corretja was seventh. But in truth, it was as predictable as a long winter in Scandinavia.

Bjorkman, with his compact strokes, remarkably quick feet, and fast-twitch volleying is a natural indoor player. Corretja, with his lengthy backswings and tendency to work well behind the baseline, is not. But Corretja, who had never lost a Davis Cup singles match until now, played with more enthusiasm than he projected before the match, ripping enough superb passing shots to extend this encounter to four sets and three hours and twenty minutes before losing 6–3, 7–5, 6–7 (5–7), 6–3.

"My finest singles match in Davis Cup," said Bjorkman, who had won the Stockholm Open in this same arena and with comparable support in 1997.

"Even if everyone thinks we were favorites in this match, we Swedish players know these guys can play even on this surface," Bjorkman said. "It was a few points here and there, but that's what you expect when you play a top 10 player like Alex."

At the time, it sounded like Bjorkman was being polite, but less than a month later in Lyons,

Corretja would become the first Spaniard to win an indoor title since 1976. In Stockholm, however, he had yet to become a believer. Oddly, neither had Moya; but he had practiced well all week, and considering his experience and established knack for thriving on big occasions, he had a much better chance of beating Johansson than Corretja did Bjorkman.

"We are here to make history," Moya said optimistically on the eve of the tie.

This was Johansson's Davis Cup debut for Sweden but not the first time he had played a role in a Davis Cup match. In 1988, when he was thirteen, Johansson was on court as a ballboy when Sweden played Czechoslovakia in the quarterfinals in Norrkoping. Sweden would win that tie, 3–2, as Stefan Edberg rallied to defeat Miloslav Mecir in the decisive rubber. "Since then, I have always followed Davis Cup," Johansson said. "And for me, it has always been a dream to be part of the team."

Johansson had earned his place by reaching the quarterfinals of the U.S. Open, beating Yevgeny Kafelnikov along the way. Two other Swedes also had reached the final eight at Flushing Meadows: Bjorkman and Magnus Larsson, the player whom Hageskog coaches regularly on tour. But Larsson had a sore wrist, and Hageskog had a hunch. Asked before the tie if he had chosen Johansson on intellect or on feeling, the Swedish captain responded, "Feeling, because I don't have intellect."

"This is Thomas's chance, and he deserves it," Larsson said. "He has been playing well the whole time lately. Calle made the right choice."

While American Davis Cup rookie Jan-Michael Gambill would struggle in his debut, the Swedish rookie would prosper against the fifth-ranked Moya, which says a lot about team Sweden's ability to integrate new components and a lot about Johansson's huge groundstrokes and textbook-ready service motion. At five-foot-eleven, he is small for a big server, but his timing and explosive leg action allow him to compensate beautifully. "We have been waiting for him to make his move," Hageskog said. "He was one of the best juniors in Europe, but it takes some time nowadays."

It would take only three sets for Johansson to give Sweden a 2–0 lead. In the past, Johansson had acquired a reputation as a player who cracks under pressure, having squandered three match points against Mark Philippoussis in the U.S. Open quarterfinals; but against Moya, with the Swedish fans for ego reinforcement, he rarely appeared vulnerable, holding his own or better from the baseline with Moya, despite the fact that Moya was generating more depth and pace than Corretja.

If there was a decisive moment, it came in the second-set tiebreaker at 2–2 when Johansson hit a second serve that Moya believed was long but which the linesmen and chair umpire viewed differently. He would lose that point and his composure: a rarity for the self-contained Spaniard. "As far as I'm concerned, chair umpires can leave the court, because all they do is sit there and agree with the linesmen," he said. "I think they have to take more risks."

After making a forehand unforced error on the next point, Moya trailed 4–2 and threw his towel in anger on the changeover. The next point would not improve his mood, as he was called for a foot-fault on his serve. He made another unforced error to trail 5–2 and lost the tiebreaker 7–4.

The Spanish exchange students who had made the short journey from the university town of Uppsala were suddenly much less boisterous, and there would be another tiebreaker in the third set. Johansson earned himself two match points with a backhand winner that gave him a 6–4 edge. Moya would save them both, the first with a backhand volley off the frame; the second with a cool and clean forehand passing shot. But Johansson would not squander three match points this time. After Moya missed a backhand volley, the Swede hit a big first serve and well-placed forehand approach and was celebrating as soon as Moya's last backhand passing shot landed out.

The tone for the Davis Cup Semifinal between Sweden and Spain was set when Jonas Bjorkman (top) defeated Alex Corretja (bottom) in the opening singles.

"I remember how I felt when I played my first Davis Cup match, so I thought he'd feel the pressure," Moya said. "But I think he showed he can be a big player in this event. It looked like it was my first match and his one hundredth."

Johansson is better at striking tennis balls than the right notes in an interview, but he was clearly overwhelmed: "I felt so tired after the first couple of games that I thought I would never make it," he said. "That was because I was so tight and nervous, but after a couple of games you feel a lot better. All I know is that going on court with a 1–0 lead has to be a lot easier than going on at 0–1."

Later that evening as Hageskog headed out the door of the press room, someone playfully called out after him, "Feeling or intellect?" Hageskog poked his head back through the doorway. "Feeling," he said with a grin.

It was no premature grin. Though the Swedes still needed one more point, the tie was essentially over, because Bjorkman and Kulti are an infinitely better doubles team than any pair the Spaniards can muster, at least as long as Moya refuses to play doubles. "I am working on him," Santana said. "I think it is just a question of time and confidence. He has the tools to be a good doubles player."

By Saturday morning, the Kunglighalle already felt more like an exhibition hall than the site of a summit meeting between two tennis heavyweights. Magnus Gustafsson had organized a "Kids Day" to help promote the sport in Sweden, and as the doubles teams prepared to face off, Corretja and Thomas Enqvist donned big black wigs and traded groundstrokes with a group of youngsters inside the arena. "Against the Spaniards, you really feel like it's a friendly match," Bjorkman said. "It feels like Davis Cup must have felt in a different time."

Bjorkman and Kulti wasted little time and few opportunities in their 6–2, 6–2, 6–2 victory over Julian Alonso and Javier Sanchez. It was domination in motion: the Spaniards did not have a single break point against the Swedes and never even managed to stretch them to deuce on their serves. Meanwhile, Bjorkman and Kulti were swinging away on their returns, poaching regularly, and getting the better of the quick exchanges at net. In little more than an hour, they improved their Davis Cup record together to 7–2 and put their nation in the Final for the third consecutive year.

This time, Hageskog's team had taken a most unconventional approach, using eight different singles players in the first three rounds, and on Saturday afternoon, all the contributors posed for Swedish photographers. "Because we are a small country, our players grow up in the same clubs and same tournaments," said Jan Francke as his team closed out its 4–1 victory on Sunday. "They know each other well, and Davis Cup is a chance for them to come together as friends."

The equally congenial Spaniards and the large Spanish press contingent that followed them to Stockholm—a larger contingent than at any other tennis event this year, including Roland Garros—will have to remain patient.

"I think Spaniards would get more excited about us winning Davis Cup than about us winning any individual titles, even Grand Slams," Corretja said.

Santana has been waiting much longer than his players: "I think I will be very unhappy if I leave this job without winning this Cup," he said. "Our generation of players created the interest in it, and the attention in Spain is much bigger than for any other event. In other countries, it is sometimes the same way. I am just very sorry and disappointed for the Davis Cup that the Americans don't play their best guys. This is something that adds nothing to the competition."

Certainly not, but it does at least create the opportunity for other nations to experience the joys

Thomas Johansson of Sweden (top) made an outstanding Davis Cup debut, defeating Carlos Moya of Spain (bottom) in straight sets in the semifinal.

of collective success. It is unquestionably more diverting to watch Italians win once in a while than Americans win all the while.

"It's not our fault if Sampras and Agassi didn't come," Gaudenzi said.

Doubles troubles

The Americans who did turn up on Saturday in Milwaukee were at least physically imposing: Martin is six-foot-six and Gimelstob six-foot-five. But they soon trailed two sets to love to Gaudenzi and Nargiso, and Italy was just one set away from hosting its first Final.

That set would not come easily, however. The Americans saved two match points in the third set on Gimelstob's serve and then won it 7–5. They then evened the match by winning the fourth set 6–2, but in the fifth Gimelstob double-faulted twice on his serve in the fourth game and was broken for the first time all afternoon. He had played and returned better than Martin for much of the match, but his inexperience was beginning to surface. "Just ashamed it had to come out in that situation," Gimelstob said. "But Davis Cup would tend to bring out your insecurities."

The Americans would break back and push Gaudenzi to deuce on his serve at 3–3. But on the next point, Gaudenzi did a fair imitation of a Squadra Azzurra goalkeeper by diving to his left for a backhand volley. Gimelstob then hit a good forehand crosscourt that Nargiso lunged for and struck for a winner down the line. "I was a little bit afraid because I did the same thing in France in 1996 and got injured and couldn't play the two days after," Gaudenzi said. "But this time it went better."

It would go badly again for Gaudenzi in the months that followed, but the Italians would hold this service game with a few fresh bruises. Gimelstob then dropped his serve once more in the next game, losing it when Gaudenzi hit a return that nicked the tape and flew past the eager New Jerseyite. It was merely the last in a long list of signs that the Americans' eighteen-tie winning streak at home was ripe for the ending. Nargiso, who had been barely treading water in the fourth set, held his serve at love in the next game and was soon lying flat on his back on the friendly court with both hands thrust in the air. He soon was gasping for air when Gaudenzi landed on top of him.

Italy was in its seventh Davis Cup Final and first since 1980, and the only people lower than Gaudenzi and Nargiso were the hosts.

"To lose 3–0 is something I certainly didn't ever dream of, and I know the players would never dream they would be in this position," Gullikson said after the doubles.

Dreams are hard to achieve when one is not at one's best, and there would be calls in the American press for Gullikson to step down and for a more iconic and influential figure (aka: John McEnroe) to assume the potentially quixotic task of convincing top Americans that team tennis matters. But McEnroe no longer sounded terribly interested: "I guess I'd have to get on my knees and beg Sampras, which is one reason I don't want to take the job," he said. "I can't imagine bending that low."

Gullikson, already director of coaching for the USTA, would keep his post and his perspective: "Believe me, I've gone through worse things, like my brother's illness," he said of his twin, Tim, who died of brain cancer in 1996. "In tennis terms, when I was on tour, I lost two matches a week just about every week. What I would say is that it's just a real honor for me to be involved in Davis Cup. Through the good times and bad times in life, that's what I do: try to stay involved."

With a very tricky first-round tie in Great Britain looming in April, Gullikson could only hope that his civic spirit would prove more contagious in Davis Cup's centennial year than it had in 1998.

The Italian team (opposite) surprised the Americans with a 4–1 defeat in Milwaukee. The decisive point came in the doubles when Andrea Gaudenzi and Diego Nargiso defeated Justin Gimelstob (left) and Todd Martin (right) to secure a place in the Final for Italy.

Andrea Gaudenzi

THE YEAR WAS 1991, and an eighteen-year-old named Andrea Gaudenzi had just arrived in Austria to train with new coach Ronnie Leitgeb and his other pupil, Thomas Muster. For their first workout session, the two men and the teenager were in the woods; Leitgeb on his bicycle and Gaudenzi and Muster jogging on foot. No more than half an hour went by before Gaudenzi sprained his ankle.

Today, Gaudenzi and the Austrians are still a year-round team, but Gaudenzi's luck with injuries has not improved. When he turned professional in 1990, the same year he won the junior championships at the French and United States Opens, more titles were expected of him. But problems with his ankles, arm, wrist, shoulder, hand, and fingers have kept him from fulfilling those expectations.

After eight years on tour, he has won only one tournament that was not a satellite or a challenger, and that victory did not come until the spring of 1998 in Casablanca. But by late summer, he was suffering again. He had to retire early in the U.S. Open because of an ankle injury, and he needed a cortisone shot to calm the pain in his chronically sore right shoulder in the Davis Cup semifinals.

"Continuity has definitely been a problem for me," Gaudenzi said of his training and tournament play over the years.

He began at age three by hitting balls against the walls inside his family's home in Faenza, which was rather normal considering that there is an abundance of racquets in his house. Gaudenzi's grandfather had founded the tennis club in Faenza, and Andrea's uncle, Stefano, was ranked as high as fourth in his country. Andrea's father was not at that level but he was an excellent club player.

He began dominating the national 12-and-under division in Italy, and at age thirteen he left home to attend boarding school near Rome so he could train at the Italian Federation's national training center. It was not an easy decision for the parents or their only son. There would be tears and fears but Gaudenzi believes that dealing with them helped him in the career that would follow.

"It made me tougher," he said. "I was in a hotel room at thirteen, which is good training for the life of a professional tennis player."

But Gaudenzi would ultimately find the federation's methods unsatisfactory: a conclusion that helped explain some of his pointed comments about Italian tennis administrators over the years. After Gaudenzi finished 1990 as the world's top-ranked junior, International Management Group arranged for him to be coached by Bob Hewitt, the combative Australian turned combative South African, who was once one of the world's finest doubles players.

This partnership would last only several months, and Gaudenzi would soon be making the trek to Vienna (and more often to Monte Carlo) to train with Leitgeb and Muster, who both put a premium on perspiration.

"After six months with them, I was completely wiped out," Gaudenzi said. "I had just one desire: to stop and go home. But I finally decided to keep going because I knew that if I could keep up with Ronnie's and Thomas's program, one of the toughest in the world, I could be one of the best players in the world."

Gaudenzi would never make it into the top 10 or past the fourth round in a Grand Slam event, but he would make remarkable progress in the rankings over the next three years, rising more than 780 spots before peaking at number 18 in February 1995. Exchanging groundstrokes daily with Muster, who would reach number one in the world the following year, certainly did not hurt.

But Gaudenzi's game would head in a different direction, and as his ranking slipped along with his health, it would be in Davis Cup that he would make the biggest impact at home. Gaudenzi might not relish the way Italy develops tennis players, but he relishes playing tennis for Italy. In 1996, he and Renzo Furlan, a childhood training partner, took Italy to the semifinals and gave their country a 2–0 lead the first day before the French rallied to win the last three rubbers.

In 1998, without Furlan and with a serendipitous draw, he would take them all the way to the Final, and anyone who watched him celebrate with Nargiso in Milwaukee knew it was the highlight of a career that has not been all it was supposed to be.

ROUND

A Capitaine for the ages surrenders the helm

AUSTRALIA d. UZBEKISTAN
Townsville, Queensland, Australia
BRAZIL d. ROMANIA
Santa Catarina, Brazil
CZECH REPUBLIC d. SOUTH AFRICA
Prague, Czech Republic
FRANCE d. ISRAEL
Tel Aviv, Israel
GREAT BRITAIN d. INDIA
Nottingham, Great Britain
NETHERLANDS d. ECUADOR
Eindhoven, Netherlands
RUSSIA d. JAPAN
Osaka, Japan
SLOVAK REPUBLIC d. ARGENTINA
Buenos Aires, Argentina
*All matches played
25–27 September, 1998*

Yannick Noah saw his French team back into the World Group before retiring as both Davis and Fed Cup captain so that he could spend more time with his young family. Preceding pages: Aussie fans go wild in Townsville.

YANNICK NOAH WAS RIDING ON HIS PLAYERS' SHOULDERS in Tel Aviv, which made for a fine but somewhat misleading picture.

First of all, this was no dramatic triumph the French Davis Cuppers were commemorating, merely a routine 4–1 victory over a young and inexperienced Israeli team in a small stadium that was never close to full. Second of all, for much of his tenure as captain, it was Noah who had lifted his players up by the force of his personality.

The French won two Davis Cups under him—the first in 1991 and the second in 1996—during a span when no French man won a Grand Slam singles title. Along the way, they made "La Coupe Davis" as affirming to their national psyche as Edith Piaf's worldly wise version of "La Vie en Rose."

It was enough to make one forgive the French for their insistence on calling Dwight Davis's silver punchbowl "le saladier." But even that was somehow appropriate, because there was certainly some metallurgy at work in all of this unexpected success. After all, what can a Davis Cup captain really influence in this era of private coaches, private planes, and a plethora of tournaments, both minor and major, that provides enough slices of the marketing-department-approved product to make even journeymen want for little?

The days of Harry Hopman, who poked and prodded and kept right on inserting shiny new components into the Australian machine, were squarely in the rearview mirror and receding fast. Authoritarianism no longer works with contemporary tennis professionals, but Noah seemed to find a new paradigm by addressing much more than forehands and backhands. There was a whiff of new age in his insistence on reaching out to the whole player by way of yoga and privation; a touch of the old school in his insistence on relying on form during practice and his own instincts to pick his final lineup.

There were often surprises on the days of the draws. The computer rankings were far too arbitrary and impersonal for "Cap'tain Yann": a man with a fine touch who also happens to like the look of his fingerprints. Captain was a part-time job for Noah, who was also busy making mediocre music and supporting his charity "Les Enfants de la Terre," but it was no sinecure. As a player, Noah never quite equaled the sum of his parts with the exception of one unforgettable spring in Paris in 1983. As a captain, his knack for math improved exponentially, although like many a natural, his attention span remained a foible.

In December 1991, Noah's team stunned the United States in Lyons to win the Cup for the first time in fifty-nine years and put France in an extremely good mood: no simple task. Less than six months later, Noah resigned after a loss to Switzerland in which he found his team's attitude lacking. He was not without blame himself, and by 1995, he was back—although no longer quite as physically involved on the bench as he had been in Lyons, when he sometimes seemed to be hitting the shots along with his companions and former rivals Guy Forget and Henri Leconte. By now, his body

and mind no longer had any interest in playing Davis Cup. He was interested in exploring the boundaries of motivating and teaching—a more multi-layered and subtly rewarding endeavor than making a serve fly to the desired corner of a box.

In 1996, when the French won it all in Malmo again, they lacked the perfect foil that the United States had represented. Beating "les 'ricains"—in a team competition the Americans had long dominated no less—was something that translated easily to the masses. Beating neutral and smaller Sweden lacked the same resonance, but this time the tennis took over from the symbolism. The plot twists were so gripping, the scores so absurdly even, and the emotion on court at the end so devoid of any artifice that Noah's team again struck a chord.

Before they rode up Les Champs-Elysees in an open car on an early winter afternoon in Paris, there was some concern that the French might not really need this traditional communion; that it had only been a tennis match after all. But the people came by the thousands.

His players would say that they were the ones who struck the shots, handled the pressure, and sweated the sweat. They were right, but Noah was unquestionably the facilitator—"the free electron," as French Tennis Federation president Christian Bimes once said.

"If Noah had not played tennis, he would still have been someone who did something out of the ordinary," said Patrice Clerc, the French Open tournament director.

An outsider might think Noah is a popular icon in France because he represents victory. After all, he was the last French player to win at Roland Garros and the captain who won two Davis Cups and France's first Fed Cup in his first year in charge of the women.

Noah is a winner. Ergo, Noah is a hero, a talisman.

But it is more complex than that in a country where the ends and the means are deeply linked. Style still counts in France. Noah has it: dreadlocks, *sotto voce*, stage presence, and all. But more intriguingly, he is infectiously enthusiastic and seemingly devoid of self-consciousness—a character trait that is about as innately French as the cheeseburger.

The French have a term for front teeth with a gap between them, the kind that Noah possesses. They call them "les dents du bonheur" (the teeth of happiness). Noah makes many of his fellow citizens feel good because he does what they don't dare to do in public: he exults, he emotes, he takes chances with his words and his reputation. And the remarkable thing—to an American at least—is that, in a nation where immigrants and outsiders are under increasing fire from the right-wing political party Le Front National, hardly anyone bothers to mention that Noah is black anymore.

This child of an interracial marriage that did not last between a Cameroonian soccer professional and a French teacher, Noah has transcended color and added a fair bit of it to a national landscape that was rather somber during much of the nineties. In general, France was in an unsettled, searching mood—short on collective goals and economic security, unsure of its place in the world, and anxious about the future. Noah seemed to have found some answers, and unlike many successful people in this self-aggrandizing era, he seemed eager to share.

"There are people in life who have charisma, and those who don't," Clerc said. "There are people in life who, no matter what they do, they attract attention. They go into a restaurant with ten people, and the eyes are on them. Yannick is like that, and he also has the ability to inspire. The French don't always believe in themselves. They have this odd capacity to believe that they are the best in the world and to doubt themselves at the same time, particularly the athletes. I think he proved to a lot of people that they can win. And I think where Noah was intelligent is that he decided to do something in which he could win; in which he could succeed and have an impact."

But Noah has the build and makeup of a sprinter, not a marathoner, and in Tel Aviv he had already decided that it was time to do something else again. This time, there had been no conflict—real or imagined—to precipitate his departure, although his relationship with Bimes had once been tempestuous and was now essentially nonexistent.

This time, it was personal. His children from his first marriage had moved to the United States with their mother, and Noah had decided to move to New York with his new family to be closer to them. He also had decided that working with the players only a few times a year in the structure of Fed Cup and Davis Cup was no longer substantive enough and that the idea of investing more of himself in French tennis was seductive (he even proposed it) but more than he could muster at this stage in his life.

"For the next two, three, or four years I want to take care of the equilibrium of my family," Noah told *L'Equipe*. "After that, if the equilibrium is good, maybe I'll come back. What is certain is that it's easier to leave in these conditions than to be fired. Since I made this decision, I feel in harmony. I feel happy to be outside of it. I'm buying myself a little bit of time. That's all."

But first he and his players wanted to put France back in the World Group. They had fallen out of it in 1997 by losing to Australia in the first round and then being bushwhacked in Belgium by a muscular substitute named Christophe van Garsse in the decisive rubber. There would be no van Garsse look-alike or play-alike in Tel Aviv; only a pair of twenty-year-olds with singles rankings in need of improvement. Harel Levy was 217 the week of the tie, Amir Hadad was 322, and though Noah does not put great stock in computers, this time the numbers were worth crunching.

Though one optimistic Israeli reporter assured Philippe Maria of *L'Equipe* that the youngsters were tenacious—"Levy can get money from a cash machine without a card"—the scorelines on Friday were even more eloquent. In the opening rubber, French number one Cedric Pioline beat Hadad 6–2, 6–3, 6–3. In the next, Guillaume Raoux handled Levy, the independent banker, with greater difficulty but in the same number of sets: 7–6 (7–1), 6–2, 6–4.

On Saturday, Raoux and partner Jerome Golmard would put both France and Israel back where they belonged with a 6–1, 6–4, 6–3 victory over Noam Behr and Eyal Erlich. Raoux and Pioline were soon carting Noah around the court, but the mood amongst the French was definitely more playful than celebratory. Raoux preserved the moment by snipping off one of Noah's dreadlocks and laying it over his lip like a moustache. Noah jokingly pretended to cry as he walked into the locker room; the page already turned. But then it must be difficult to feel the sharp pain of separation when a team already has reached its collective goals.

"I'm proud of all that I accomplished as a player and captain," Noah told *L'Equipe*. "But in the end, what counts is the way people look at you, and I know that I got much more respect from others as a captain than as a player."

Rule Britannia?

Other Davis Cup nations have their goals in front of them: none more than Great Britain, which had fallen out of the World Group in 1992 by losing to Leander Paes and India and was finally in position to rejoin it by defeating Leander Paes and India.

A great deal had changed in those six years, including Greg Rusedski's address. In 1992, the

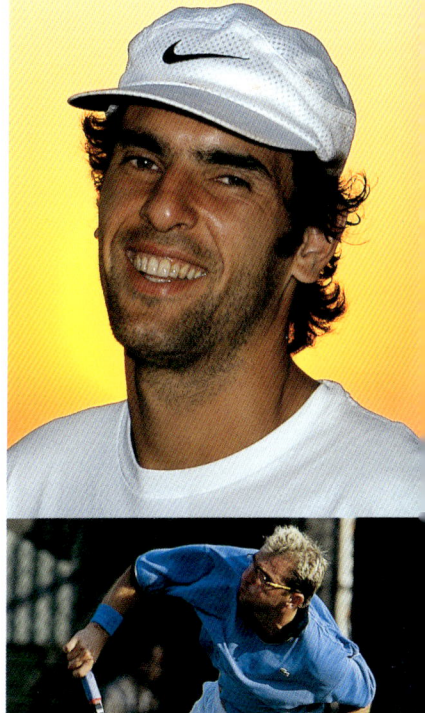

The victories of Cedric Pioline (top) and Guillaume Raoux (bottom) accounted for France's first two points in the World Group Qualifying Round against Israel without the loss of a set. Raoux completed the French victory by winning the doubles with Jerome Golmard.

British team had deserved to start dropping, and it struck bottom in 1995 when it was beaten by the Slovak Republic in Bratislava in Group Two of the Euro/African zone. The Slovaks were better at the time than most casual observers realized, but the British then had to beat Monaco—much more famous as a tax haven for talent than a developer of talent—in order to avoid dropping into the netherworld of Group Three.

It would be Rusedski's first tie after deciding to leave Canada and play for Britain, the nation in which his mother was born but not raised. Ignominy would be averted by the reassuring score of 5–0. But 1995 would not just be the year Rusedski discovered the delights of waving the Union Jack at Wimbledon and beyond. It would also be the year that David Lloyd took over as captain and the year that a truly local boy, Tim Henman, would begin to flash his considerable potential.

One of the world's best doubles combinations, Leander Paes and Mahesh Bhupathi of India, defeated Olympic silver medalists Neil Broad and Tim Henman of Great Britain in straight sets in the World Group Qualifying Round.

If everyone had been healthy, the suddenly powerful Britons should have returned to the World Group in 1998, but in the first round of Group One against Zimbabwe in 1997, both Rusedski and Henman missed the tie with injuries. Byron and Wayne Black gave the Zimbabweans the victory, which only made it clearer that the Britons have two world-class players and no more.

Henman and Rusedski would have to wait, and the waiting finally brought them to a medium-fast hardcourt outdoors in Nottingham and a return engagement with Paes, who has long made a habit of playing better for his populous country than for himself. "Leander and Davis Cup for some reason go together," Rusedski said.

His Davis Cup singles record upon arrival in England was 23–14 and his victims over the years have included Goran Ivanisevic, Wayne Ferreira, Jan Siemerink, and, in one particularly memorable long weekend against France in 1993, Henri Leconte and Arnaud Boetsch.

"I think if we make it 1–1 after the first day coming into the doubles, we have a hell of a shot at the tie," said Paes, who was ranked third in the world in doubles with partner Mahesh Bhupathi.

Paes would very nearly grant his own wish against Rusedski in the opening rubber, which would last three hours and sixteen minutes and surely felt much longer than that to Rusedski, who often struggled with his confidence against an opponent who likes to attack as much as he does. Lloyd had chosen to play the tie on a hardcourt instead of on grass, because even if grass was Henman's and Rusedski's favorite surface, it was also Paes's favorite. There is a growing feeling among captains that it is best to go with your own strength no matter what the opposition likes, and second guesses were certainly flitting through British brains as Paes got to match point on his serve in the fifth set.

But Rusedski saved that match point with a backhand return that hit the netcord and tumbled over for a winner. "I got a little bit fortunate but sometimes you deserve a little bit of luck," said Rusedski, who missed Wimbledon this year with an ankle injury and was still not completely fit.

At the U.S. Open, Rusedski had played five-set matches in the first three rounds, finally losing to Siemerink and dropping out of the top 10 for the first time in nearly a year because of it. But to Rusedski's credit, he was still mentally and physically solid enough to eke out a 1–0 lead for Britain with a 2–6, 6–3, 3–6, 6–2, 11–9 victory.

"For a while it was just a question of hanging in there, but I managed to get away with it," Rusedski said. "And that's the best you can hope for when everything is not firing on all cylinders."

Henman would also misfire early, but he would require much less time to find his rhythm against the 368th-ranked Bhupathi, winning 4–6, 6–3, 6–3, 6–3. "The first set was just a matter of one or two missed shots but there was no reason to panic," Henman said. "I know I have been playing well lately."

The British win would set up the perfect match: a date with the U.S. in the Centenary year.

Greg Rusedski (left) and Tim Henman (right) have put British tennis back on the map and into the elite Davis Cup World Group for the first time since 1992.

The 11th-ranked Henman, a semifinalist at Wimbledon, had been playing very well, and he would play well again in Saturday's doubles. The problem was that his thirty-one-year-old partner, Neil Broad, could not return the favor or the Indians' serves with any great success. Lloyd had determined that Rusedski needed time to recover from Friday's marathon. Henman and Broad had beaten the Indian team on their way to the silver medal at the 1996 Summer Olympics, but Paes and Bhupathi have become more accustomed to each other's faces and games since then. It showed in all three sets, which the Indians won 7–6 (7–2), 6–3, 7–6 (7–3).

Britain still needed one more point to make its point, and if Paes had been fresh, he might well have made Henman suffer more to prove it. There was still plenty of flash and opportunism from the Indian, one of the more consistently spectacular players on the circuit. But Henman, who grew up in a country with a dearth of tennis role models in the professional game, looked very much like one as he remained focused despite the pressure.

"Definitely the best Davis Cup match I've played," he said after the pressure had been relieved in straight sets.

Paes often appeared to be hurting: he was treated for a sore right shoulder and was favoring what would turn out to be a bruised left heel as he walked about between points. Henman viewed this as a tactic, not a symptom.

"What he was trying to do was a pretty good idea: serving without much pace and walking as if he can't move could have been a distraction, but I was not going to be distracted," he said.

John Roberts, the *Independent*'s often wry tennis correspondent, put it differently: "If Paes was on his last legs, any number of the competitors in the Nottingham marathon would have traded with him."

Henman was still in command, but England being England, he could not do much about the weather. It began to drizzle, and in the third set with Paes leading 4–3, referee Gabriel Mato inspected the court but decided that play could continue. "It's easy for the referee to say it's all right, because he's not the one who's going to run around and slip on the lines," Henman said later.

But this would not be an overcast day dominated by British complaints, and play continued to a tiebreaker, which Henman won with a forehand volley that might not have been heard around the world but was certainly heard at home. After six years in the wilderness, Great Britain was back in the World Group, and for a nation with an acute sense and appreciation of history, it was a timely result with 1999 being the centennial of Davis Cup.

The event had begun in 1900 because the Americans and Dwight Davis fancied the idea of challenging Great Britain, the nation that had codified the modern game. They were the only two nations to play in that inaugural year, and when the draw for 1999 was held in October, symmetry was well served. Great Britain would host the United States in the first round in April.

It was unclear whether the best Americans would deign to play, but one hundred years after the world's premier team tennis competition was launched, it was abundantly clear that the best Britons still cared.

"It's been a long, hard road but mission accomplished so far," said Lloyd. "Now we have to see if we can go further."

So do the Russians, who have never won the Davis Cup but who have never had two extremely talented singles players in their lineup until now. Yevgeny Kafelnikov already has won a Grand Slam event: the 1996 French Open. Marat Safin, at age eighteen, should be in the hunt in the years to

Russia defeated Japan 3–1 in the World Group Qualifying Round. Russian teenager Marat Safin (top) posted his first singles win in the competition, defeating Takao Suzuki of Japan (bottom). With balletic grace to match his intensity, Gustavo Kuerten (opposite) led Brazil to a 3–0 victory over Romania.

come. In what was essentially his debutante ball, Safin pushed Jim Courier to five sets and lost in the decisive rubber against the Americans in the first round. He then proved that was no fluke by reaching the fourth round at the French Open and U.S. Open.

Against the Japanese in Osaka, Safin would get his first two Davis Cup victories as the Russians won with relative ease, clinching the victory on Saturday when Kafelnikov and Safin combined to defeat Gouichi Motomura and Takao Suzuki in four sets. The final score would be 3–1 Russia because the final reverse singles match was cancelled because of rain.

More rain and a trip to Spain

With Argentina leading 2-1, Slovak Republic's Karol Kucera (top) and Dominik Hrbaty (bottom) won both of their singles on the final day to secure a place in the 1999 World Group.

Rain would also force the cancellation of the last two matches on Gustavo Kuerten's home island of Santa Catarina in Brazil. But by that time, the Brazilians already had assured themselves of a third straight year in the World Group by defeating the Romanians, 3–0, without losing a set.

The Brazilian team featured the same players who had lost to Spain at home in April, but the administration was new and indicative of a trend. The Belgians Filip Dewulf and Johan van Herck already had forced a change at the top of their Davis Cup hierarchy by having their private coaches take control. Now, the Brazilians had essentially done the same thing. Paulo Cleto was out as captain, and Ricardo Acioly, who coaches Fernando Meligeni, was in, along with Kuerten's coach Larri Passos, who would serve as Acioly's assistant.

"Paulo was a very good captain but he sometimes put many pressures on the players," Passos said. "He was just working for Davis Cup, not traveling the rest of the year with the players. Acioly and I do, and I think that takes some of the pressure off. We are looking at the whole season, not just the Davis Cup week.

"I think after we lost to Spain in the first round, Gustavo was mentally very down, and I tried to talk with him and tell him that it was important to just play relaxed and enjoy playing again. But his mentality was destroyed, so we talked to the president of the federation and we asked to put in a new program. He agreed, and I could feel the difference after the tie against Romania. Usually after Davis Cup, the players are very tired, not just physically but mentally. But this time it was different. If Gustavo won the tournament in Mallorca right after Davis Cup, it was not a coincidence."

Kuerten has proved he can win in Spain, and in 1999, he will get another chance to prove it, because the Brazilians and Spaniards will play again in the first round. So will the Swedes and Slovaks, but only because Miloslav Mecir and the Slovaks managed to survive a major threat on clay in Buenos Aires. Karol Kucera might have had a remarkable season, breaking into the top 10 and beating Pete Sampras at the Australian Open and Andre Agassi at the U.S. Open. But he very nearly lost all three of his rubbers against the Argentines.

After Dominik Hrbaty gave Slovakia a 1–0 lead by defeating Franco Squillari in straight sets, Hernan Gumy handled Kucera with stunning ease, 6–1, 6–1, 6–4. Kucera and Hrbaty were then beaten in doubles in straight sets by Lucas Arnold and Luis Lobo, which meant the Slovaks—who led the Swedes 2–0 in the first round—needed to sweep the reverse singles to avoid returning to Group One.

Their predicament was a clear reflection of the increasing depth in the men's game, and when Kucera blew a two-set lead against Squillari, it appeared that Argentina might be returning to the World Group for the first time since 1992. But Kucera won the fifth set to complete a 6–3, 6–3, 3–6,

6–7 (3–7), 6–4 victory. Hrbaty, who had lost the decisive rubber to Magnus Gustafsson in Bratislava in April, handled a similar situation much more successfully, defeating Gumy, 6–2, 3–6, 6–4, 6–2.

The Dutch and Czechs would have a much less trying time in qualifying. The Dutch were again without number one Richard Krajicek who had reinjured his knee at the U.S. Open, but the other moving parts of their potentially formidable team, including Paul Haarhuis and Jan Siemerink, were healthy this time, and the Dutch swept Ecuador, 5–0, in Eindhoven. The Czechs may be permanently without their number one, Petr Korda, who has announced and not yet reconsidered his retirement from Davis Cup, and they figured to have some difficulty in Prague against Wayne Ferreira and the South Africans. But the clay-court surface suited singles players Bohdan Ulihrach and Slava Dosedel a great deal better than the visitors, who appeared far from inspired anyway. The Czechs would win 5–0, dropping only twenty-four games in thirteen sets, which was enough to cost South African captain Danie Visser his job.

No blunder down under this time

The Australians also won 5–0, defeating Uzbekistan indoors in Townsville, a seaport in Patrick Rafter's home state of Queensland. Rafter, who had not played a professional event in Queensland since he was a teenager, was naturally the main attraction: all the more so because he had just defended his U.S. Open title in grand style in New York.

Despite the fact that most Australians probably could not locate Uzbekistan on a map, the forty-eight-hundred-seat indoor stadium was sold out for all three days.

"Tennis is on a high in Australia," captain John Newcombe said. "What I hear from the tennis coaches is that business is up; that their camps for kids are sold out; that more people are coming back and playing and that night tennis is into a rebirth."

While Pete Sampras, one of the men Rafter had beaten to win the Open title, had declined to play at home for the United States in the semifinals, Rafter had flown through many time zones to play at home in the much less gratifying qualifying round. Despite some nagging tendinitis in his left knee that would later force him to end his season early, he even played a dead rubber on Sunday after Mark Woodforde and Todd Woodbridge had clinched the victory the day before with a 6–3, 7–6 (7–3), 7–6 (7–4) defeat of Oleg Ogorodov and Dmitri Tomashsevich.

Ogorodov is a former member of the Soviet junior team that also developed Yevgeny Kafelnikov and Andrei Medvedev. He has an impressive physique and serve, but neither he nor his teammates could keep the Australians from sweeping every set contested in Townsville. It was an exorcism of sorts, and as Linda Pearce, tennis correspondent for the *Age* in Melbourne, pointed out, "Townsville was what Mildura should have been: Davis Cup competition against an unheralded team brought to a tennis-starved regional center" with Australia and its U.S. Open champ and excellent doubles team winning comfortably despite the absence of Mark Philippoussis.

But Philippoussis and the calamitous, cacophonic first-round loss to Zimbabwe in Mildura had definitely not been shoved into some Freudian closet. It remained a topic before, during, and after the rout in Townsville: "I think all of us who were in Mildura suffered for a number of weeks after-ward," Woodforde said. "It wounded all of us."

"We were sort of surrounded by negativity," Newcombe said. "We all believed we were positive and ready to go, but I've got this theory, and experience shows this: if you are surrounded by the neg-

The Netherlands returned to the World Group with a 5–0 victory over Ecuador. Two points in the tie were contributed by Jan Siemerink (top). Slava Dosedel (bottom) of Czech Republic played a key role in the 5–0 defeat of South Africa. Czech Republic will continue its streak of nineteen consecutive years in the World Group, a record shared with Italy and Sweden.

The Aussie destiny: will they redeem themselves next year in Harare and grow stronger?

Fresh from his second U.S. Open victory, Aussie Patrick Rafter (left) traveled to Townsville, Queensland, to take part in his country's 5–0 victory over Uzbekistan. He was joined by Jason Stoltenberg (right) who played second singles for the Australian team.

ative, it's very hard to get those negative vibes out of your system."

There had been more negativity at the U.S. Open, where Philippoussis had finally broken through in a major event, reaching the final against Rafter. It was the first all-Aussie final in a Slam since 1976, and Davis Cup coach Tony Roche had decided to sit in the front row of Rafter's box during the match. That did not sit well with Mark or his father Nick.

"I was extremely disappointed," Philippoussis said. "I expected a lot more. I should have known a lot better."

For Roche, the issue was clear: "I'm the Davis Cup coach, and I'm responsible for the players in the Australian team," he said after the match. "I'm not just talking about Pat. I also coached Jason Stoltenberg, Scott Draper, and Lleyton Hewitt here."

Philippoussis was certainly not a member of the team, but he was a member of the Olympic Athlete Program, another group that Roche oversees for Tennis Australia. Roche, disturbed by the uproar, would later threaten to abandon his Davis Cup duties, which set in motion a chain of threats: from Newcombe, who said he would not continue without Roche; to Rafter, who said he would not continue without Newcombe and Roche. By the time everyone left Townsville, it was clear that everyone planned to continue except Philippoussis.

By early October, after Philippoussis informed Tennis Australia president Geoff Pollard of his plans by telephone (but not Newcombe or Roche), it was clear that everyone was on board for 1999. It was a pleasant surprise, but after regaining their equilibrium without Philippoussis, it will be intriguing to see if the Australians can regain their hallmark cohesiveness with him back in the line-up and the locker room.

"In the whole time that this has blown up, Tony and I have never said a bad word publicly about Mark," said Newcombe, who had sent Philippoussis a fax after the victory over Uzbekistan. "We believe he's a good kid and that the ability is there for him to be top five in the world. We've said that for the last five years, and now it's up to Mark to make that commitment and fulfill his potential, and we're happy to do anything we can that's possible."

What the draw for 1999 would make possible were an inordinately high number of rematches, and as chance would have it, the team the reunited Australians will face in the first round is again Zimbabwe. This time, they will have to travel to Harare: exactly what Zimbabwe Tennis Association president Paul Chingoka had humbly suggested they do in 1998 in the interest of promoting the sport in his part of the world.

"Maybe that's destiny," Newcombe said of the draw. "Maybe we're destined to redeem ourselves and grow stronger because of it."

The mustachioed Australian who has yet to experience the same success in Davis Cup as a team leader that he did as a leading player paused for a moment, thinking back on all the unexpected twists and scores of the last six months.

"Or maybe they are destined to beat us both home and away," he said with a laugh.

Tim Henman

ASK TIM HENMAN which sporting accomplishment he most admires and he does not talk about someone winning a tennis tournament. Instead, he talks about a team: the English soccer team that won the World Cup on its own soil in 1966.

"Obviously I wasn't around," said Henman, who was born in 1974. "But I can really relate to the pressures of winning in your own country."

Not since the 1930s, when Fred Perry was hitting his forehand on the run and looking dapper in the process, has a Briton won Wimbledon. Not since Perry was the leader of the British team in the same decade has Henman's nation—the nation that codified and first excelled at the modern game of tennis—won the Davis Cup.

Henman, the slender and artful man from Oxford, is now in position to change all that. He will have the chance at Wimbledon, where he was a quarterfinalist in 1996 and 1997 and a semifinalist in 1998, losing to his friend and occasional dinner partner Pete Sampras in four high-quality sets.

Henman may have another chance next December in the Davis Cup Final. But only if he and Greg Rusedski can get the best of the American team—with or without Sampras—that will travel to Birmingham for a first-round tie that is both symbolic and contemporary.

"The regard for the Davis Cup in the U.K. is, I think, right up there with Wimbledon," Henman said.

Henman knows it is not the same on the other side of the Atlantic, which makes for a poignant role reversal as the century draws to a close. In 1900, when Dwight Davis started the competition, the Americans were the ones urging the British to send their best players. They did not comply: Laurie and Reginald Doherty remained at home, and the British lost at Longwood Cricket Club in Boston.

In 1999, it is the British who are urging the best Americans to come. "We want the Americans to field their strongest team," Henman said. If the Americans do not, and Sampras already has announced that he will not play Davis Cup in 1999, the chances are excellent that they will suffer the same fate as the Britons in 1900. Henman knows more about tennis history than most of the modern stars. His family is part of it. His great grandmother, Ellen Mary Stowell Brown, was the first player to serve above the shoulder at Wimbledon, and his grandmother, Evelyn Susan Billington, was the last to serve underhanded. His grandfather, Henry Billington, played Davis Cup for Britain immediately after the war in 1946 and holds a career Davis Cup record of 1–1 in doubles.

Billington's grandson already has improved on that, but Henman admits to a certain degree of nostalgia-fatigue in a nation where the past is impossible to ignore as you walk through its ancient streets and villages. "People are always asking me about my tennis background, but honestly, it doesn't have any relevance to why I play the game," he said.

As evidence, Henman points to his two older brothers, neither of whom became tennis players, but he unquestionably comes from a household where tennis was accessible. He learned to play on a private hardcourt at the house his parents purchased in Oxford. At age five, he was already at Wimbledon watching and admiring Bjorn Borg.

Borg transformed himself into an attacking player by necessity at the All England Club, but for Henman, no transformation is necessary. With his fluid serve and volleys and innate taste for risk, he is a natural grasscourt player. "One day he's going to win this thing; I can tell you that," Sampras said after his victory in the 1998 Wimbledon semifinals.

Henman has had a chance to mingle frequently with the man who, like Borg, has already won it five times. Henman and his coach, David Felgate, like to dine with Sampras and his coach Paul Annacone when they are on the road. Henman also has learned from Stefan Edberg, another smooth mover with a yen for the net with whom he practiced frequently for several years in London. It remains to be seen whether Edberg helped develop a player who can help Britain put an end to Sweden's hold on the Davis Cup.

FINAL ROUND

A one-act opera in Milan

SWEDEN d. ITALY
Milan, Italy
*All matches played
4–6 December, 1998*

BEFORE THE 1998 DAVIS CUP FINAL BEGAN, in ordinary fashion, with a draw, there was a chance to take an extraordinary stroll. Across the Piazza del Duomo, with the late Gothic, intricately carved cathedral as a backdrop. Into the Galleria Vittorio Emanuele II, where the refurbished Davis Cup had been on display earlier in the week under the soaring, fin-de-siècle arcades. Back outdoors and into the Piazza della Scala, home to the mother of all opera houses and home, as well, to the Palazzo Marino: seat of Milan's city government.

For the first time since Dwight Davis created his team competition, the Davis Cup Final had come to Italy, and on this crisp December morning as the Final's principal performers filed into an antechamber of the Palazzo, the grandeur of central Milan stood in stark contrast to the status of the singles players.

The teams with stars in (or out of) their lineups, including the United States, Australia, and Spain, had failed to advance this far. The stage in Milan—a fine city for stages—had been left to the lesser lights, which was excellent for the Italians and Swedes but less reaffirming to the prestige of the Davis Cup as it prepared to fete its centenary year.

It is a venerable event, a routinely gripping event: a warm gust of communalism and benign nationalism in the midst of a generally cool, capitalistic, and every-man-and-agent-for-himself climate. It has an important role to play in the game but role players would play a disproportionately large role this December.

Sweden and Italy have impeccable Davis Cup credentials: along with the Czech Republic, they are the only nations not to have been relegated since the World Group was formed in 1981. But for the first time since the advent of the computer rankings in the early 1970s, not one of the four men chosen to play singles in the Final was ranked in the top 30. And not one of the four—not Magnus Gustafsson and Magnus Norman for Sweden and not Andrea Gaudenzi and Davide Sanguinetti for Italy—had advanced past the quarterfinals in a Grand Slam event.

Unlike the Italians, the Swedes and their clever captain, Carl-Axel Hageskog, had other options. Though Magnus Larsson and Thomas Enqvist were out with injuries, they still had Thomas Johansson, now ranked 17th after an excellent second half of the season, and Jonas Bjorkman, currently the most successful Swedish Davis Cup player and already a member of two winning teams in 1994 and 1997.

But Hageskog is not a man who lives and decides by the rankings. Unlike other teams with less depth, there are no guaranteed spots in the Swedish lineup. Hageskog watches practice closely. He considers the surface and the states of mind, and there was a lot to consider as he and his players gathered in Monte Carlo to prepare for the Final on Côte d'Azur red clay that would prove considerably slower than the indoor clay court the Italians would ultimately lay down.

From Bjorn Borg to the present generation, the Swedes have long frequented Monte Carlo and

The ITF used the 1998 Final to announce plans for next year's Davis Cup Centenary in an on-court ceremony that had as its showpiece the priceless one-hundred-year-old trophy.

its income-tax-free streets and practice courts. But though they were in the principality on business this week, they found time for pleasure, as well, and pleasure for the Swedes usually means mischief.

"You make a joke and then someone makes one on you; that's the way it works with us," said Bjorkman, who once fell for a dinner invitation from a Bjorn Borg impersonator named Peter Lundgren. "There are a lot of things you have to be careful of," Bjorkman said, shaking his head.

Hageskog has certainly learned to be careful over the years, but when his portable telephone rang eight days before the Final, he did not think twice when a female voice told him she was calling on behalf of Prince Albert of Monaco, a tennis fan and former Olympian who would be delighted if the Swedish team would accept his invitation to dinner.

Hageskog told his caller that he did not want to be impolite but he would have to consult with his players. The players, surprisingly, were all in favor of the idea, even if it did mean dressing up for the occasion. Several hours later, they were up in the old city and heading for the palace entrance with Captain Hageskog leading the way.

"Calle was walking in like he was this proud matador," Gustafsson said.

But the matador would soon discover that he was not walking on a red carpet. A guard interceded brusquely: "You can't pass here."

Captain Hageskog pointed at the palace and replied in a slightly slighted tone, "But he invited us to dinner."

"I think we were all scared to say something at that point, but finally we had to say something," Gustafsson said.

They also had to begin laughing and not stop for quite some time. The prince's female assistant had been an employee in the ATP Tour office in Monte Carlo; the devious minds behind the prank belonged to Bjorkman and his doubles partner, Nicklas Kulti. Dinner would have to be eaten elsewhere than in the company of royalty.

"I have to admit; it was very well done," Hageskog said. "I have fooled them too many times, so it was time for me to get fooled also. But I'm going to get them back, and I won't tell them how."

Somehow, they still find time for tennis

This is how Team Sweden functions in private, and there is no arguing with its results in public: Davis Cup champions in 1994; semifinalists in 1995; finalists in 1996; champions in 1997; and finalists again in 1998.

This year, their individual results had not been exceptional. Though Johansson, Bjorkman, and Larsson had all managed to reach the U.S. Open quarterfinals in September, no Swede had finished in the top 10 for the first time since 1973. Collectively, however, they remained formidable as well as risible.

On Team Sweden, there are frequent jokes, or "yokes" as Hageskog calls them in his excellent but still Swedish English. There is a week-long event, conceived and coordinated by Hageskog for more than a decade, called the "Star League," in which he gives daily grades to his players during Davis Cup rounds: grades that have very little to do with logic and a lot to do with Lewis Carroll–style levity.

"If somebody forgets his pants or shoes, he's punished," Hageskog explained. "And the boys have great fun reading this everyday. I buy some stupid prizes, and it's prizes and surprises for them. Whenever I see people like Mats Wilander and Joakim Nystrom, who used to be on the team, they want to know who won the league. You can get five stars for something: that's world class. The worst is a crossed star, and the great thing is you can get five stars for one thing one day and a crossed star for the same thing the next day. I try to keep them guessing."

There is also the more serious and quantifiable matter of the Sports Quiz, a roadtrip staple, which pits the players against the coaches and allows questions about all sports from the past century and at which everyone is competitive except Johansson, who would rather watch *Friends* than football. "He doesn't help us players out much there," Bjorkman conceded. "He's not a sports maniac like me or Larsson."

For the more physically inclined, there is also the annual post-season hockey game between players and coaches, a game at which everyone is competitive except Johansson, who is not much of a skater. "He's still a junior on the skates," said Larsson, who, like Bjorkman, is not.

One might wonder how the Swedes knew so much about Johansson, who only made his official Davis Cup debut in September against Spain in the semifinals. But growing up together is part of the Swedish system, and young men like Johansson and Norman are brought into the team as practice partners long before they are ready to contribute as front-line players.

"It's important to let them grow slowly into the team so they see what it's all about," Hageskog said.

It is partly about healthy competition, and as the Swedes competed against each other on the Monte Carlo clay, it soon became clear that one of the singles players was going to be Gustafsson, the hero of the first-round comeback against the Slovak Republic and the oldest member of the team at age thirty-one.

"He was playing incredibly in practice," said assistant captain Anders Jarryd.

Johansson would ultimately fall out of contention because of his relative weakness on clay and because of patellar tendinitis in his knee. Arriving in Monte Carlo after his teammates did not help his cause. "I had the feeling that he wasn't really going for it 100 percent; that he wasn't sure about himself and his knee," Hageskog said.

But Bjorkman, despite being traditionally ill at ease on clay, was confident and focused enough to make a serious run at a single spot. Fresh after eight days of vacation in Antigua and Barbuda in the Caribbean, he made Hageskog and Jarryd think hard before finally deciding that Norman would be their second man and that Bjorkman would have to settle for being a doubles specialist.

"During the time I've been on the team with Calle the last four years, picking this second singles spot was the most difficult decision," Jarryd said.

The way it was decided says a lot about the Swedes' consensual approach to management. Hageskog has long made a habit of announcing his lineups to his players on the eve of the draw, and on Wednesday, he called Norman into his room to consult with him and Jarryd. "If I tell him, 'I want you to play,' and he says, 'Yes but the others are good,' then I know he's not ready," Hageskog said. "So I wanted to talk to him first, and then I wanted to see what Jonas and Nicklas Kulti thought. They are the veterans. But Norman is a fine young man because he told me that he wanted to play, but only if the other players agreed that he should play so that everyone would be behind the decision."

Despite Norman's mediocre season, everyone appeared to agree that his affinity for clay-court tennis and his hustling, aggressive-baseline style were convincing arguments in his favor. When the Swedes arrived at the Palazzo Marino on Thursday, they were all advocating the common cause.

"I support the decision 100 percent," said Johansson, despite the fact that he has always gotten

Italian captain Paolo Bertolucci (top) looked to the heavens for inspiration when his number 1 player, Andrea Gaudenzi, was forced to retire in the opening match while Swedish captain Carl-Axel Hageskog reflected on the comfort zone that Sweden's depth of players brings to the Davis Cup.

the better of Norman in singles matches dating back to their junior days. "And let me tell you something else, we're going to win. It's tough to see how they can beat Gustafsson on this surface. Norman is playing well, and we have an extremely strong doubles team with Bjorkman and Kulti."

The less holistic hosts

The Italians were not exuding the same sense of manifest destiny. There had been conflict between the players and the Italian Tennis Federation over money and over the future of captain Paolo Bertolucci, who had been operating on unflatteringly short-term contracts all season and had yet to be reconfirmed for 1999 despite Italy's first run to a Final in eighteen years.

The players wanted Bertolucci to be rewarded and supported, but the federation, hesitant because of internal dissent, was unable to satisfy the players or Bertolucci before the Final began.

The condition of Italy's best player and team leader, Gaudenzi, now ranked 44th, was also less than satisfactory. He had not played an official match since he had finished off the Americans in late September and celebrated by pouncing on doubles partner Diego Nargiso. On October first, he had undergone arthroscopic surgery to alleviate chronic pain in his right shoulder. He had resumed practicing at the end of October and cancelled plans to play on the ATP Tour's South American swing. Though he now claimed to be "110 percent," two months away from competitive tennis represented a potentially destabilizing break in this era of high work rates.

"Obviously I'd be happier if I had played a lot of tournaments and won many matches, but that's not the case," he said. "The only thing I can say is that a Davis Cup match is a different thing. Hopefully with the help of the crowd, I'm going to get into the match very quickly."

In truth, the crowd was the most imposing face card in a weak Italian hand. Italians no longer follow tennis with nearly the same intensity as when Nicola Pietrangeli and Adriano Panatta were at their peaks in decades past. But national teams continue to strike a chord, and the Davis Cup squad's largely inexplicable success in recent seasons—quarterfinalists in 1995 and semifinalists in 1996 and 1997—had given the competition visibility and Italian players a welcome dose of celebrity that their mediocre tour results were not about to generate.

In 1997, the oft-injured and lowly ranked Omar Camporese had become something of a hero by leading Italy to an upset of Spain in the quarterfinals. This year, Gaudenzi and Sanguinetti had done better yet, and though the locals will never care as much about Gaudenzi and Sanguinetti as they do about Inter and AC Milan, they cared enough to buy Davis Cup tickets in bunches.

All of the three-day tickets for the Final were sold in early November, and on the eve of the Final, only a few hundred single-day tickets remained available: all in the upper reaches of the twelve-thousand-seat Forum, an ungainly modern arena which, with its polychromatic external tubing, looks like a poor cousin of Paris's Centre Pompidou and a destitute cousin of central Milan's architectural splendors.

But at least the Milanese would get the chance to see Davis Cup. They had not had that opportunity in thirty-three years: not since a second-round zonal match against Brazil in 1965. Milan once had been a haven for the Italian team—Milan's own Fausto Gardini never lost a match there during his fine career—but it had been a suspiciously long separation: one that could be explained, in part, by the tension that existed between former Italian federation president Paolo Galgani and the regional league in Lombardy.

It was very noisy in Milan's Forum as local fans (top) gathered to support their team in the first Davis Cup Final ever staged in Italy, while a much smaller group from Sweden (bottom) cheered their side to victory

But Galgani had been replaced in late 1997 by Francesco Ricci Bitti, and Milan was non grata no longer. For the Swedes, Milano was also a city with a tennis past: not all of it pleasant. In 1957, they had come to Milan for the European Zone semifinals and lost 4–1 to a team led by Giuseppe Merlo and Pietrangeli, who defeated Ulf Schmidt in the fourth rubber to clinch the victory after an Italian umpire made a horrific call on a Schmidt serve at a crucial point in the second set.

Swedes with shorter recall might remember what happened farther south in the final of the Italian Open in 1978 when Borg threatened not to finish his match against Panatta if Italian fans did not stop throwing coins in his direction. At least Borg had managed to win that match.

Overall, the Italians held an 11–7 edge over the Swedes in Davis Cup, but they had beaten them only once in their last five meetings and had lost convincingly in the 1997 semifinals in Sweden when Bjorkman had won all three of his matches indoors and played a particularly overwhelming doubles match with Kulti against Camporese and Nargiso.

"I think Sweden has a bit better chance than us here," Bertolucci said. "But remember, it was the same situation against the United States in the semifinals, and look what happened."

This would be Italy's seventh Davis Cup Final. Its previous six had all been played on the road and it had won but once: in 1976 by defeating Chile 4–1 on clay in Santiago with Panatta and Corrado Barazzutti playing singles and Bertolucci playing doubles with Panatta, who also won the French Open that year. All three men were on hand for Thursday's draw in the Palazzo Marino, but intramural relations were not at an all-time high.

In 1997, shortly after the upset victory over Spain, Panatta resigned because of a disagreement with President Galgani. Barazzutti had been asked to replace him but had declined in a show of solidarity with Panatta. Bertolucci, who was without a coaching job at the time, ultimately accepted the post, which reportedly irked Panatta.

With Galgani out of power, Panatta was now national technical director. Barazzutti was also in Milan as a television commentator, and some members of the Italian federation were pushing him as a replacement for Bertolucci as captain. But despite the internal tensions and the Italian gift for "la polemica," all three former teammates did agree that this Final was a precious opportunity to rekindle interest in the sport.

"I think this is really a very important moment for the base of tennis in Italy," Barazzutti said on the day of the draw. "We need to increase the number of youngsters playing the sport in this country because we have a lot of older people who play but not so many children anymore. I hope this Final will catch the young people's fancy."

That would depend on the result, and as the draw concluded and the buffet tables were quickly picked clean and the Italian players walked in the direction of their chauffeured courtesy cars in the Piazza della Scala, they posed for photographs in their blue overcoats and blue ties in front of a statue of former Milan resident Leonardo da Vinci.

The Swedes did the same, and at the Forum over the next three days, they would come considerably closer to producing a masterwork than the Italians.

The crowd did not know that yet, of course, and when the two teams walked on court on Friday, there was enough enthusiasm to make the Italians feel a lot better than their rankings. There were airhorns blasting and other more ancient forms of noise as the Italians were introduced, and as the din continued, Gustafsson, who was standing nearby, glanced at the tips of his sneakers and grinned.

"If you're going to play on the road, it might as well feel like you're playing on the road," he

Five hours and five sets into the match, a sudden, sad ending to Italian dreams.

The momentum in the opening match of the 1998 Davis Cup Final shifted from Sweden's Magnus Norman (top left) to Italy's Andrea Gaudenzi (second from left, top) and back again but, after achieving a tremendous comeback in the fifth set, Gaudenzi was forced to retire to Norman because of a torn shoulder tendon.

would say later.

For most of the four hours and fifty-seven minutes that Norman required to give Sweden a 1–0 lead, the crowd and the banners dangling inside the arena were much more diverting than the tennis.

There was the erudite: a quote from Dante's *Divine Comedy* that read, "Abandon all hope, ye who enter here."

There was the considerably less erudite: a quote from a Milanese fan that read, "I like Swedish girls."

Others prefer marathon matches

But Davis Cup has long made a habit of transforming mundane encounters into memorable encounters, and that habit was not broken on day one of this Final. By the time the opening match reached a climax abruptly and, believe it or not, prematurely with Gaudenzi in great pain and Norman in great spirits, the two error-prone and robust baseliners had the undivided attention of everyone in the building.

The two players already had something in common: a disquieting medical history. Gaudenzi had been operated on twice on his right shoulder, one of the most important joints in a tennis player's body. Norman's problems have been with his heart. He has suffered from arrhythmia and had to be treated on court because of it when he played Goran Ivanisevic at Wimbledon in 1997.

"It's a valve problem," Norman explained. "Some people here might have the same problem, but they don't notice it because they are not professional athletes and are not putting their body under that kind of stress."

A year before, Norman had undergone surgery on his heart to ameliorate his condition. He had scheduled it for the day after the 1997 Final in Gothenburg just in case Hageskog selected him for the team. He had not been chosen and as his teammates celebrated their lopsided victory over the Americans, Norman spent six hours in an operating room in a Gothenburg hospital. It was not an open-heart procedure. Instead, it required the insertion of a tube into his body that allowed surgeons to manipulate the errant valve.

"It's absolutely better now," Norman said in Milan. "In my mind, it's made a big difference. As a tennis player, you don't want to think about something like that." Four months after the operation, Norman had made his Davis Cup debut in another hostile indoor clay court environment in the first round against the Slovak Republic, losing in five sets to Dominik Hrbaty and then defeating Kucera in five sets in one of the best matches of the Davis Cup season to keep Sweden's hopes alive in Bratislava. But he would find a way to fail more often than succeed in the months that followed, and instead of building on his fine 1997 season he struggled and dropped thirty spots in the rankings to 52. His only good results had come at minor clay court events: he reached the final in Croatia and won the event in Amsterdam.

Like Bjorkman, who nearly chose ice hockey over tennis in his teens, Norman also had a difficult decision to make as a youth. He could get serious about tennis or serious about bandy, a variation of field hockey that is popular in Sweden.

"Bandy was my biggest sport until I was fifteen, but I also had quite a lot of success in tennis from the beginning," he said. "But at fifteen, I had to choose between the national junior team in bandy and the national junior team in tennis. The bandy team was going to Russia and the tennis team was going to Florida."

Norman understandably followed the sun, but he does not come from a traditional tennis hotbed in Sweden. His town of Filipstad and the state of Varmland in which it lies are better known for producing writers and poets than Davis Cuppers.

"For me, it's absolutely the biggest thing you can do in life, play for your own country," Norman said. "And it's something I am always going to do, whether I'm number 1, 2, or 50 in the world. If Calle wants me, I'll be there for him."

That is the sort of comment Tom Gullikson seldom gets to hear, but Norman made Hageskog suffer for his loyalty in Milan by making him sit and sit and sit through one of the most nerve-racking encounters of the season.

The first set required sixty-eight minutes before Gaudenzi won it 11–9 in the tiebreaker, and he won it with considerable help from Norman, who made two forehand unforced errors when he held set points in the breaker. When another Norman forehand sailed long to give Italy a one-set lead, Gaudenzi hunched over and pumped his fists like he had just won a tournament.

In the second set, Gaudenzi broke Norman early and then took a 3–0 lead with a service winner that both Norman and his captain thought had landed out. Perhaps they were simply searching for an edge with Gaudenzi in control, but the Swedes need not have worried. Neither player would prove capable of sustaining consistency or dominance in this uneven match. In the next game, Gaudenzi double-faulted twice and lost his own serve. When the set went to a tiebreaker, Norman made quick work of it, 7–0, and when Gaudenzi lost the last point on a forehand error, the Swedish players and entourage were on their feet: a wave of joy in a vast and eerily tranquil sea.

It would not remain calm for long: Gaudenzi, with the help of a backhand winner off the frame of his racquet, broke Norman in the seventh game of the third set and then served it out. But what Norman did not know was that Gaudenzi was feeling pain in his post-operative shoulder.

"It started a little bit in the middle of the second and then got really bad in the middle of the third," he said.

But he would not take an injury timeout until after Norman had evened the match by pushing forward with greater frequency and winning the fourth set. By then, they had been playing for three hours and forty-two minutes, but Gaudenzi used up several more minutes than he was legally allotted as he received an extensive shoulder massage at courtside. Norman, who was having his powerful thighs rubbed by trainer Per Bastholt, looked fragile himself, but he would quickly—and speed was relative in this match—jump out to a 4–0 lead in the fifth.

After losing his serve for the second time, Gaudenzi hurled his racquet to the clay. "He seemed to be very, very tired," Norman would say later.

But Gaudenzi was still very, very aware that playing a Davis Cup Final in his own country was probably a once-in-a-career opportunity. Despite the pain, he began to come to net more often himself, perhaps because it was not making his shoulder feel any better to sit back and exchange wrenching groundstrokes with Norman.

"I couldn't play the forehand as I wanted to play it," he said. "I could only play cross-court, never down the line. I was limited the whole match; I was probably 60 percent of what I can play normally."

Nonetheless, he held serve with ease, then broke Norman to get back to 4–2. He held serve again with ease, smashing a jump overhead à la Sampras, to get back to 4–3 and put the airhorns back in full service. But the clearly nervous Norman did not let him get even, at least not yet. When Norman takes his racquet back for a forehand, it looks like he is preparing to hit a much heavier object than a ball. That may explain why the Swede is error-prone off that wing, but when in great need he came up with a bolt of a forehand winner to hold his serve and stay ahead: 5–3.

After Gaudenzi held at love, Norman served for the match, the crowd completely drowning out his teammates. It would be the best game of the match and although nobody knew it yet, the best game of the long weekend. Gaudenzi took a 15–40 lead. Norman then won the next three points at the net to earn a match point, which Gaudenzi saved with a forehand winner that must have hurt more than most: It was down the line.

With the score at deuce for the third time, Gaudenzi dived to his left and hit a desperate backhand volley. Though Norman lunged forward, he could not reach the shot and both weary men ended up lying on the clay. It was clear by now that both their hearts were in working order, and Gaudenzi would win the next point with a short backhand winner to even this most even match at 5–5.

What you Swedish viewers missed

Who cared anymore how pedestrian the tennis had often been in the first four sets? This was transcendent stuff and with no fifth-set tiebreaker, there was no end in sight. Or was there? On the final point of the next game, Gaudenzi cracked a first service. As Norman's return missed its target, Gaudenzi immediately hunched over at midcourt. At first, it appeared he was merely expressing the same sort of intense delight he had expressed after winning the opening set. But it soon became clear that he was in intense pain.

"I felt something go crack in my shoulder," he said.

The crack was the sound of a tendon ripping, and as he walked to his seat with twelve thousand Italians watching him in person and millions more on national television, he wore an expression of frustration and resignation. As he sat on his chair during the changeover, he grimaced and rotated his arm in its socket with the help of a trainer. What had been sore was now all but useless.

"I couldn't even lift a cup," he said.

Gaudenzi lifted himself out of his chair and returned to the court but it was all postscript now. Norman held at love to make it 6–6. Gaudenzi then gamely attempted to serve. He lost the first point when Norman greeted his soft second serve with a huge forehand return winner. In the middle of the next exchange, the Italian stopped playing altogether, shook his head and trudged toward the net to retire.

"I played with the pain for five hours, and I could stand it, but at that stage the pain was just too big," Gaudenzi said. "I tried to hit the ball, but it was completely impossible."

Norman had prevailed by the most unconventional score of 6–7 (9–11), 7–6 (7–0), 4–6, 6–3, 6–6, and when the two men reached the net after their mutual ordeal, they embraced and exchanged compliments and condolences.

"I felt very, very sorry for Andrea because he was playing an unbelievable match," Norman said. "I was a little bit surprised when he broke me twice in the fifth, but he had the crowd behind him, so I guess the power came from the crowd."

What was particularly impressive about Norman's performance was his ability to keep his composure amidst the ruckus. "Normally, I have a very bad temperament, but today I was trying to be calm all the time, no matter what happens, to try not to think about the crowd and just look at my Swedish teammates," he said.

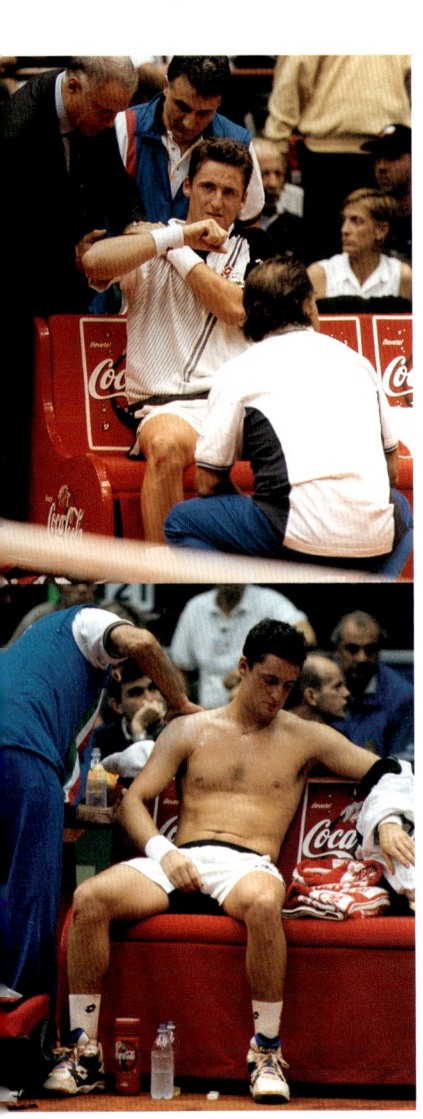

Andrea Gaudenzi (top and bottom), who had undergone shoulder surgery after Italy's defeat of the Americans in the Semifinals, played his first official match against Magnus Norman in the opening singles of the 1998 Final. Nearly five hours later, Gaudenzi was again facing surgery, as a shoulder tendon had torn during the match.

Hageskog had attempted to prepare his players for the Italian fans during their stay in Monte Carlo by asking them what Borg, Wilander, and Stefan Edberg all had in common. The correct answer was that they were calm on court.

"They could handle the stress in matches, and I asked my players if they wanted to be in that same kind of company," Hageskog said. "I think Norman did a terrific job of concentrating instead of thinking about the fans or the linesmen. It's a pity the way the match ended, but it was a fantastic fight."

A fantastic fight that Swedish viewers did not get to see live from beginning to end. With Norman leading 5–4 in the final set, Swedish public television left the match to broadcast a regional news program. Swedish fans would have to wait until a highlights program that began at 10 p.m. that evening to watch the conclusion. To an outsider, it seemed a remarkably poor decision and was widely criticized in the Swedish press, but it came at a time when the ITF Davis Cup Committee was lending an increasingly receptive ear to calls to reduce Davis Cup singles matches to best-of-three sets. A match that should have been an ode to the five-setter was instead an exhibit for the prosecution.

"It just leads home to the fact that we have to try to contain the matches into some sort of reasonable period," ITF president Brian Tobin said.

"It is great: five hours like that, but you have to be a real tennis follower," Committee member and former Australian captain Neale Fraser said. "It would be very interesting to see the number of people who sat down and watched that match without leaving the TV; I bet it would be very few. So you've got to at least look at change."

One also could argue that if the match had lasted only three sets, those who had deigned to watch it would have no reason to remember it. But there is no watertight argument in this debate, which has the potential to divide tennis into hostile camps in the years ahead.

Norman and Gaudenzi already had parted ways. Norman was still a player; Gaudenzi was now a patient and would undergo more shoulder surgery the Monday after the Final. His surgeon would be Christian Schenck, the same Austrian doctor who already had operated on him twice and whose previous clients included skiers Thomas Sykora, Marc Girardelli, and Anita Wachter and Swiss tennis player Martina Hingis.

Those are fine names to drop, but the question is whether Gaudenzi should have played at all in Milan. "We were in contact with the doctor who did the surgery all the time," Bertolucci said. "All the practices were under the control of the doctor. Andrea was ready."

Gaudenzi and his coach, Ronnie Leitgeb, agreed. "Andrea was dying to play here," Leitgeb said. "He was fine in practice beforehand but the thing you can't predict is the stress of competition and the effect of that stress."

According to Leitgeb, Gaudenzi would have needed more surgery after the season anyway. "It was a question of having the major surgery after the USA semifinal and missing this or having minor surgery and having a chance to play," Leitgeb said. "There was still a slight tear in the tendon before the match, but we really believed it could hold up."

For the third straight year, an injury had knocked a key player out of the Davis Cup Final. In 1996, it had been Edberg, although that had hardly affected the drama in Malmo when the French beat the Swedes, 3–2. But in 1997, when Sampras had torn a calf muscle in his opening singles match, his injury had destroyed the competitive balance and created a rout. This year would be no different; the Italians had counted on Gaudenzi for at least two points. Now, he would account for none.

"It's as if all the luck that got Italy to the Final has run out," Pietrangeli said.

Restless nights = routine victory

It would have taken a great deal of good fortune for Sanguinetti to change the course of the day's second singles match. "My game is based on emotions, and unfortunately my game was affected by Andrea's injury," Sanguinetti said.

But even on an emotional high, it is difficult to imagine how he could have solved the riddle of Gustafsson's enormous forehand. While the opening match had been an epic, this was nothing more than a short feature. Gustafsson would win, 6–1, 6–4, 6–0, in well under two hours, which may explain why Swedish television was able to show all of this match.

The two players—Norman and Gustafsson—who had kept Sweden in the Davis Cup in the first round by sweeping the reverse singles on the road had now put Sweden within very close range of their third Davis Cup title in five years. And Gaudenzi was no longer available to play doubles with Nargiso. "For me Gustafsson has always been not my idol but a mentor," Norman said. "Without him noticing it, I think he has taken care of me in Bratislava and also here."

For Gustafsson, a caring sort who has helped form an organization called "Tennis Future" to help promote the junior game at home, it was a particularly emotional moment. Though he had not played for Sweden in the quarterfinals or semifinals, he knew as soon as Italy defeated the United States that his chances of being in the team for the Final were excellent.

"I was thinking about that almost the whole time, and at the beginning of the indoor season I wasn't playing that well because I was thinking too much about it. Finally, I just relaxed because I realized that if I kept playing like that I wasn't going to be in the Final anyway. But I must admit that in the last week, I have been very nervous."

So nervous that he had trouble sleeping for several nights before the match. "I was a little bit afraid about Gustafsson because he was so eager to take advantage of his chance that he was almost overdoing it in the practice sessions," Hageskog said. "But I think the problem got solved, and I think we all believed that we owed Magnus this Final. He has been helping us all out for ten years, and this was his chance."

Gustafsson might have had his chance earlier if not for chronic problems with his shoulder (Gaudenzi can relate). But since reaching number 10 in the rankings in July 1991, he has never managed to scale quite the same heights.

"All I know is that if they had Grand Slam events on indoor clay, he would have won one," Hageskog said. "This surface is what suits his game best."

The Italians are better known for their affinity for outdoor clay: the sort that covers the courts at the Foro Italico. The court in Milan played quicker than they would have liked, partly because it was laid directly on concrete and could not be watered as heavily as a court with a dedicated irrigation system. But Gaudenzi's injury had made the court speed irrelevant, and now Bertolucci would have to use Sanguinetti and Nargiso in doubles for the first time together on Saturday.

"We need a lot of miracles," Bertolucci conceded glumly late on Friday evening.

None would be forthcoming, and on Saturday, a day so clear that the Alps stood in sharp and magnificent relief on the horizon, the Italians returned to the danker confines of the Forum to face Bjorkman and Kulti. But first, there would be an on-court ceremony with Boris Becker and Pietrangeli, two of the Davis Cup ambassadors selected by the ITF to help commemorate the event's Centenary in 1999. As Becker and Pietrangeli walked on court to a very warm reception, the lights dimmed and

Playing in the first Davis Cup Final of his long career, Sweden's Magnus Gustafsson (top) devastated Italy's Davide Sanguinetti (bottom), who was also making his Final debut.

sparklers planted in the clay sent flames spewing into the air. Another flame spurted out of the Cup itself, but there would be no way to brighten up what was left of this forgettable Final.

Grab sneaker, then grab doubles partner

It would remain mildly compelling for forty-five more minutes. That was how long the Swedes needed to win the opening set in a tiebreaker, 7–6 (7–1). It was not a typically solid Bjorkman and Kulti performance, perhaps because they never had played a match on indoor clay before. Though they won their first four service games without losing a point, when Kulti served for the set at 5–4, the Italians broke him after he went for too much on a first serve at 30–40 and then, after his second serve, gave Nargiso a short forehand he could drive for a winner.

Kulti would be the weaker link in the Swedish chain throughout the afternoon: Bjorkman would not face a break point on his serve in the match and was his typically explosive self. But the overall quality of the Swedish returns and the relative weakness of Nargiso's serve and Sanguinetti's deuce-court instincts (he had never played there before) would soon make a big difference in the score.

The Swedes won the second set 6–1, and were soon up 5–3 and 30–40 on Nargiso's serve in the third set. Bjorkman would squander the first match point, proving a bit too eager on a forehand return off a second serve to the body. But the Swedes soon had another match point, and this time, Bjorkman did not misfire off a second serve. His backhand return landed crosscourt for a clean winner, and for the second consecutive year, he and Kulti had the honor of clinching the Swedish victory in the Final.

The year before, it had come against Todd Martin and Jonathan Stark in Gothenburg, but Bjorkman's reaction was not about to change. He reached down and gleefully grabbed the toe of his right sneaker with his right hand. The "Brusselstep," an arcane and ungainly move acquired from watching a Swedish comedy troupe called Galenskaparna, has gotten plenty of use in the last two seasons, and Sweden now stands alone.

Since the World Group was formed in 1981, Sweden has reached eleven Finals in eighteen years and won six titles: more than the Americans, the Australians, or any of the other teams with longer but not deeper connections to this competition.

"Yes, the Swedes do have good singles players but their biggest weapon is their harmony, their chemistry," said Becker as he watched Kulti and Bjorkman perform on Saturday.

One hopes that the rest of the tennis world's main attractions were paying attention along with Becker. "We are always going to play Davis Cup because we feel it's great for us and it's something we all really enjoy," Bjorkman said. "But it would be even better if we had the chance to beat the best."

In 1997, the Swedes had beaten the best opponent possible. In 1998, they had to settle for defeating a team of opportunists, but in the end, the Italians seemed nearly as divided as they did conquered. On Saturday, the issue of Bertolucci's future resurfaced dramatically in the form of verbal attacks and counter-attacks from the players and federation officials.

"We think Bertolucci must be reconfirmed, maybe even for two or three years more," Nargiso said. "If he's not here with us, we won't be here either."

There was also an exchange of unpleasantries between Gaudenzi and Ricci Bitti, who share the

Sweden's Nicklas Kulti (top) celebrates his team's victory over Italy as he and partner Jonas Bjorkman defeated Davide Sanguinetti and Diego Nargiso (bottom) of Italy. Kulti and Bjorkman also won the decisive point in the 1997 Final over the United States and were congratulated by Captain Carl-Axel Hageskog (opposite).

Camaraderie plus comedy. It is the Swedish way. The way that gave this nation its seventh cup.

The champions Sweden are the undisputed leaders in Davis Cup, not just for 1998, but also since the World Group was introduced in 1981. Above, from left, Magnus Gustafsson, Nicklas Kulti, Thomas Johansson, Magnus Norman, Jonas Bjorkman, and Captain Carl-Axel Hageskog

same birthplace, Faenza, but not the same opinions. Gaudenzi expressed disappointment that Ricci and Panatta had not watched all of his match from courtside and did not call him afterward to check on his condition or congratulate him for his effort.

"At the end of the match, they seemed very happy," he said. "But the worst thing is that at the opening ceremony, they applauded the Swedish players but not us. They didn't even cheer for us. They probably saw twenty minutes of my match."

That meant they missed a lot, but Ricci Bitti and Panatta dismissed their best player's attacks. "What does he want? He shouldn't even have played. Andrea thinks he's like Ronaldo but for me he's like Colonnese," said Ricci Bitti, referring to one of soccer star Ronaldo's lesser known teammates on Inter Milan.

"I've been a player and I know what Andrea's feeling, but I think he should learn how to behave," Panatta said.

Ricci Bitti, who said he had sent a messenger to compliment Gaudenzi, also took another dig at his nation's top player: "I understand he went to a discotheque afterwards; maybe it wasn't so bad after all," he said.

There was more repartee with an edge in a news conference on Sunday in which Ricci Bitti again declined to give Bertolucci a vote of confidence. It was only later in December that he finally confirmed that Bertolucci would remain the captain in 1999, although the range of his responsibilities would be reduced to on-court matters.

Whatever other decisions were forthcoming, what happened in Milan was unquestionably a missed opportunity for Italian tennis to project itself as a modern and mobilized force. And the Italian disarray only made the Swedes look more remarkable.

Dead rubbers and a lively celebration

On Sunday, after Gustafsson had beaten Gianluca Pozzi and Nargiso had beaten Norman in the two, now-meaningless reverse singles, the Swedes gathered around the Cup to take possession of it for the seventh time in their small nation's history.

"What can I say? I will never win a Grand Slam, but besides a Grand Slam, this is the best you can win," Gustafsson said. "When I finish my career, I will know that I created something, and to do it together with all my friends is an even better feeling."

The friends formed a circle around the punch bowl. They raised it high in the air as the photographers snapped and the Italian fans departed, but the friends really could have used more room. Though five Swedish players were in Milan, three others also had won points for the team in 1998. There had been Tillstrom and Larsson in doubles in Bratislava in the first round. There had been Enqvist in singles in Hamburg in the quarterfinals.

It was enough to make Hageskog's thank you speech a long one, and when he had finished, Anders Jarryd walked on court with a bottle of champagne and passed it around from player to player, friend to friend. Kulti used his turn to pour champagne on Hageskog's head, and Gustafsson was soon twisting his captain's wet hair into original and, better yet, embarrassing designs as the cameras clicked away for posterity.

Camaraderie plus comedy. It is the Swedish way, and one look at the record book will confirm that it is the right way as a century of Davis Cup draws to a close.

Carl-Axel Hageskog

SCAN THE DAVIS CUP RECORD BOOK and you will find no trace of Carl-Axel Hageskog as a player. Unlike many of the other World Group captains—including John Newcombe, Manuel Santana, Miloslav Mecir, and several others—Hageskog was never good enough to represent his country at the highest level. Instead, he settled for becoming a world-class coach, and since joining the Swedish Davis Cup team in 1985, he has played enough roles and worked enough ties—forty-nine in all entering the centenary year—to have as fine a grasp of what Dwight Davis had in mind as any of his more celebrated counterparts.

He has been called Gandhi by his high-spirited players because, Swede or no Swede, he bears a faint resemblance to the man. He was called Albert by his players at the 1998 Davis Cup Final for reasons that will become clear if you peruse the final chapter of this book.

But above all, he is Calle: short for Carl-Axel and appropriately informal on a team where keeping one's distance is not the rule. "If you don't have a sense of humor with this group, you might as well just turn around and go home," said Swedish Tennis Association president Jan Francke, the man who promoted Hageskog to captain in 1995 after John-Anders Sjogren retired.

Home for the Hageskogs and their two young daughters is in Vaxjo, a small, unassuming southern Swedish town that is best known for its glassworks and may have produced more tennis stars per capita than any community except Bradenton, Florida.

The best to come from Vaxjo was the first: Mats Wilander, who developed his game at Vaxjo Tenissalskjap when the club had only one indoor court. There are now three, along with four outdoor courts—hardly enough to get a rally started in the most renowned tennis factories. But then this is no factory. It is a place for craftsmen/coaches like Hageskog, and in Wilander's wake, the club's finest handiwork has included Jan Gunnarsson, Niclas Kroon, and two of Hageskog's Davis Cup regulars: Magnus Larsson and Jonas Bjorkman.

Hageskog hardly spends the bulk of his year in Vaxjo. He travels the circuit full-time as Larsson's personal coach, but he still finds time to devote to the club and help coach its team during the Swedish championships. Both Larsson and Bjorkman play for Vaxjo, and in 1997 they and Hageskog helped win the Swedish club title shortly before winning the Davis Cup in Gothenburg.

It all makes for a great deal of togetherness. "We know each other so well; we're always training together or out doing something together like golf or ice hockey," Bjorkman said. Bjorkman has occasionally differed with Hageskog over lineup choices, but personnel decisions—he made some particularly astute choices in 1998—and player relations are generally Hageskog strengths. He tries to call each of his team members every Monday all year round. "I don't think of them as tennis players; I think of them as friends," Hageskog said. "And I want them to be able to talk to me about anything that's on their minds."

Hageskog first saw Larsson at a practice session when Larsson was fourteen: "I had never seen anyone who could hit the ball so hard when I tossed it to him so lightly," Hageskog said. "I thought he had something special."

His opinion has not changed, and he and and his private pupil have, thus far, adequately juggled a potentially awkward situation. "Of course a few journalists think it's strange, but if you look at it, the same situation exists in other teams, too," Hageskog said.

The difference is that other teams, such as the Slovak Republic, where captain Mecir also coaches Kucera, do not have as much competition for spots in the lineup as Sweden. But Hageskog often has kept Larsson on the bench: the 1998 semifinals against Spain are the most recent example, and he plans to continue making choices as Davis Cup captain through the year 2000. Any opponent who hopes that two titles in two years is enough to make the Swedish captain complacent did not hear his 1999 game plan shortly after his victory in Milan. "This year, we had Magnus Norman and Magnus Gustafsson in the Final, and they were very motivated," he said. "But I think next year Thomas Enqvist and Thomas Johansson will be important players for me. I would like to see Enqvist win a Final because he has been important for Swedish tennis, and he has yet to win one." Fellow centenary contestants, be warned.

World Group

FIRST ROUND
3–5 April

Sweden defeated Slovak Republic 3–2, Bratislava SVK
Dominik Hrbaty (SVK) d. Magnus Norman (SWE) 7–6(5) 4–6 6–4 3–6 6–2
Karol Kucera (SVK) d. Mikael Tillstrom (SWE) 1–6 6–1 6–2 6–4
Magnus Larsson/Mikael Tillstrom (SWE) d. Martin Hromec/Jan Kroslak (SVK) 6–2 6–3 6–4
Magnus Norman (SWE) d. Karol Kucera (SVK) 6–3 4–6 6–3 3–6 6–3
Magnus Gustafsson (SWE) d. Dominik Hrbaty (SVK) 6–2 5–7 7–5 7–6(4)

Germany defeated South Africa 5–0, Bremen GER
Nicolas Kiefer (GER) d. Grant Stafford (RSA) 4–6 4–6 6–1 6–2 6–2
Tommy Haas (GER) d. Wayne Ferreira (RSA) 7–6(2) 3–6 6–3 6–4
Boris Becker/David Prinosil (GER) d. David Adams/Ellis Ferreira (RSA) 5–7 6–4 6–4 6–3
David Prinosil (GER) d. Wayne Ferreira (RSA) 6–4 6–7(4) 7–6(4)
Tommy Haas (GER) d. Grant Stafford (RSA) 6–1 7–6(4)

Spain defeated Brazil 3–2, Porto Alegre BRA
Gustavo Kuerten (BRA) d. Carlos Moya (ESP) 5–7 1–6 6–4 6–4 6–4
Alex Corretja (ESP) d. Fernando Meligeni (BRA) 4–6 6–4 3–6 6–4 6–4
Gustavo Kuerten/Jaime Oncins (BRA) d. Alex Corretja/Javier Sanchez (ESP) 6–1 7–5 3–6 6–2
Alex Corretja (ESP) d. Gustavo Kuerten (BRA) 6–3 7–5 4–6 6–4
Carlos Moya (ESP) d. Fernando Meligeni (BRA) 7–6(4) 6–2 6–2

Switzerland defeated Czech Republic 3–2, Zurich SUI
Bohdan Ulihrach (CZE) d. Ivo Heuberger (SUI) 6–7(7) 6–0 7–5 6–2
Marc Rosset (SUI) d. Daniel Vacek (CZE) 3–6 6–2 7–6(5) 6–0
Lorenzo Manta/Marc Rosset (SUI) d. Martin Damm/Daniel Vacek (CZE) 6–4 6–7(5) 4–6 6–1 6–4
Marc Rosset (SUI) d. Bohdan Ulihrach (CZE) 6–4 7–5 7–5
Martin Damm (CZE) d. Ivo Heuberger (SUI) 7–6(3) 5–7 7–6(5)

Italy defeated India 4–1, Genoa ITA
Andrea Gaudenzi (ITA) d. Srinath Prahlad (IND) 6–0 6–2 1–6 6–2
Mahesh Bhupathi (IND) d. Davide Sanguinetti (ITA) 6–4 6–4 6–4
Andrea Gaudenzi/Diego Nargiso (ITA) d. Mahesh Bhupathi\Fazaluddin Syed(IND) 6–3 6–4 3–6 6–3
Andrea Gaudenzi (ITA) d. Mahesh Bhupathi (IND) 6–1 7–6(3) 6–1
Davide Sanguinetti (ITA) d. Srinath Prahlad (IND) 6–2 6–3

Zimbabwe defeated Australia 3–2, Mildura AUS
Jason Stoltenberg (AUS) d. Wayne Black (ZIM) 6–3 6–4 5–7 7–5
Byron Black (ZIM) d. Patrick Rafter (AUS) 3–6 6–3 6–2 7–6(0)
Todd Woodbridge/Mark Woodforde (AUS) d. Byron Black/Wayne Black (ZIM) 6–4 7–6(6) 6–2
Wayne Black (ZIM) d. Mark Woodforde (AUS) 6–3 7–5 6–7(3) 6–4
Byron Black (ZIM) d. Jason Stoltenberg (AUS) 6–2 3–6 6–3 6–4

Belgium defeated Netherlands 3–2, Brussels BEL
Jan Siemerink (NED) d. Johan Van Herck (BEL) 6–4 6–3 4–6 6–1
Filip Dewulf (BEL) d. Sjeng Schalken (NED) 7–5 6–2 7–5
Jacco Eltingh/Jan Siemerink (NED) d. Filip Dewulf/Libor Pimek (BEL) 6–1 6–4 6–4
Filip Dewulf (BEL) d. John Van Lottum (NED) 6–4 6–0 6–4
Christophe Van Garsse (BEL) d. Sjeng Schalken (NED) 6–4 6–4 3–6 3–6 6–3

USA defeated Russia 3–2, Stone Mountain, GA, USA
Yevgeny Kafelnikov (RUS) d. Jim Courier (USA) 6–2 5–7 6–7(2) 6–4 6–4
Andre Agassi (USA) d. Marat Safin (RUS) 6–3 6–3 6–3
Todd Martin/Richey Reneberg (USA) d. Yevgeny Kafelnikov/Marat Safin (RUS) 7–6(3) 6–1 2–6 6–1
Yevgeny Kafelnikov (RUS) d. Andre Agassi (USA) 6–3 6–0 7–6(3)
Jim Courier (USA) d. Marat Safin (RUS) 0–6 6–4 4–6 6–1 6–4

QUARTERFINAL ROUND
17–19 July

Sweden defeated Germany 3–2, Hamburg GER
Tommy Haas (GER) d. Jonas Bjorkman (SWE) 7–6(4) 7–5
Thomas Enqvist (SWE) d. Nicolas Kiefer (GER) 6–3 6–3 7–5
Jonas Bjorkman/Nicklas Kulti (SWE) d. Boris Becker/David Prinosil (GER) 4–6 7–6(5) 7–6(5) 6–4
Jonas Bjorkman (SWE) d. Nicolas Kiefer (GER) 6–3 4–6 6–2 5–7 6–4
Tommy Haas (GER) d. Magnus Larsson (SWE) 6–7(4) 7–5 6–2

Spain defeated Switzerland 4–1, La Coruna ESP
Carlos Moya (ESP) d. Ivo Heuberger (SUI) 6–1 6–2 6–1
Alex Corretja (ESP) d. Marc Rosset (SUI) 6–1 6–2 6–2
Lorenzo Manta/Marc Rosset (SUI) d. Julian Alonso-Pinter/Javier Sanchez (ESP) 3–6 6–3 6–4 5–7 6–2
Carlos Moya (ESP) d. Marc Rosset (SUI) 7–5 6–1 7–5
Alex Corretja (ESP) d. George Bastl (SUI) 6–0 7–5

Italy defeated Zimbabwe 5–0, Prato ITA
Andrea Gaudenzi (ITA) d. Wayne Black (ZIM) 6–3 6–3 6–4
Davide Sanguinetti (ITA) d. Byron Black (ZIM) 6–3 6–3 6–0
Andrea Gaudenzi/Diego Nargiso (ITA) d. Byron Black/Wayne Black (ZIM) 1–6 7–5 7–5 6–3
Diego Nargiso (ITA) d. Genius Chidzikwe (ZIM) 6–0 6–2
Davide Sanguinetti (ITA) d. Wayne Black (ZIM) 6–4 3–6 6–3

USA defeated Belgium 4–1, Indianapolis, IN, USA
Jim Courier (USA) d. Filip Dewulf (BEL) 6–3 7–6(1) 2–6 6–3
Andre Agassi (USA) d. Christophe Van Garsse (BEL) 6–2 6–2 6–2
Jim Courier/Todd Martin (USA) d. Xavier Malisse/Johan Van Herck (BEL) 5–7 6–2 6–7(2) 7–6(5) 6–1
Todd Martin (USA) d. Xavier Malisse (BEL) 7–6(1) 6–3
Christophe Van Garsse (BEL) d. Jim Courier (USA) 3–6 4–1 ret.

SEMIFINAL ROUND
25–27 September

Sweden defeated Spain 4–1, Stockholm SWE
Jonas Bjorkman (SWE) d. Alex Corretja (ESP) 6–3 7–5 6–7(5) 6–3
Thomas Johansson (SWE) d. Carlos Moya (ESP) 7–5 7–6(4) 7–6(6)
Jonas Bjorkman/Nicklas Kulti (SWE) d. Julian Alonso/Javier Sanchez (ESP) 6–2 6–2 6–2
Jonas Bjorkman (SWE) d. Carlos Moya (SWE) 6–3 7–5
Julian Alonso (ESP) d. Thomas Johansson (SWE) 6–1 7–6(3)

Italy defeated USA 4–1, Milwaukee, WI USA
Andrea Gaudenzi (ITA) d. Jan-Michael Gambill (USA) 6–2 0–6 7–6(0) 7–6(4)
Davide Sanguinetti (ITA) d. Todd Martin (USA) 7–6(0) 6–3 7–6(8)
Andrea Gaudenzi/Diego Nargiso (ITA) d. Justin Gimelstob/Todd Martin (USA) 6–4 7–6(3) 5–7 2–6 6–3
Gianluca Pozzi (ITA) d. Justin Gimelstob (USA) 7–6(4) 7–5
Jan-Michael Gambill (USA) d. Davide Sanguinetti (ITA) 4–6 6–3 6–3

FINAL ROUND
4–6 December

Sweden defeated Italy 4–1, Milan ITA
Magnus Norman (SWE) d. Andrea Gaudenzi (ITA) 6–7(9) 7–6(0) 4–6 6–3 6–6 ret.
Magnus Gustafsson (SWE) d. Davide Sanguinetti (ITA) 6–1 6–4 6–0
Jonas Bjorkman/Nicklas Kulti(SWE) d. Diego Nargiso/Davide Sanguinetti (ITA) 7–6(1) 6–1 6–3
Magnus Gustafsson (SWE) d. Gianluca Pozzi (ITA) 6–4 6–2
Diego Nargiso (ITA) d. Magnus Norman (SWE) 6–3 6–2

QUALIFYING ROUND FOR 1999 WORLD GROUP
25–27 September

Australia defeated Uzbekistan 5–0, Townsville AUS
Patrick Rafter (AUS) d. Oleg Ogorodov (UZB) 6–3 6–3 6–4
Jason Stoltenberg (AUS) d. Vadim Kutsenko (UZB) 7–5 6–1 6–0
Todd Woodbridge/Mark Woodforde (AUS) d. Oleg Ogorodov/Dmitri Tomashevich (UZB) 6–3 7–6(3) 7–6(4)
Patrick Rafter (AUS) d. Dmitri Tomashevich (UZB) 6–2 6–4
Jason Stoltenberg (AUS) d. Oleg Ogorodov (UZB) 6–3 6–3

Brazil defeated Romania 3–0, Santa Catarina BRA
Fernando Meligeni (BRA) d. Adrian Voinea (ROM) 6–1 6–4 7–6(3)
Gustavo Kuerten (BRA) d. Andrei Pavel (ROM) 7–5 6–3 6–3
Gustavo Kuerten/Jaime Oncins (BRA) d. Andrei Pavel/Gabriel Trifu (ROM) 7–5 6–4 6–4
Gustavo Kuerten (BRA) v Adrian Voinea (ROM) - abandoned due to rain
Fernando Meligeni (BRA) v Andrei Pavel (ROM) - abandoned due to rain

Czech Republic defeated South Africa 5–0, Prague CZE
Slava Dosedel (CZE) d. Wayne Ferreira (RSA) 6–2 6–3 6–4
Bohdan Ulihrach (CZE) d. Marcos Ondruska (RSA) 6–1 6–2 6–1
Jiri Novak/David Rikl (CZE) d. Wayne Ferreira/Piet Norval (RSA) 6–4 6–2 6–2
Bohdan Ulihrach (CZE) d. David Nainkin (RSA) 6–0 6–1
Slava Dosedel (CZE) d. Piet Norval (RSA) 6–1 6–1

France defeated Israel 4–1, Tel Aviv ISR
Cedric Pioline (FRA) d. Amir Hadad (ISR) 6–2 6–3 6–3
Guillaume Raoux (FRA) d. Harel Levy (ISR) 7–6(1) 6–2 6–4
Jerome Golmard/Guillaume Raoux (FRA) d. Noam Behr/Eyal Erlich (ISR) 6–1 6–4 6–3
Harel Levy (ISR) d. Cedric Pioline (FRA) 3–6 6–1 6–2
Nicolas Escude (FRA) d. Amir Hadad (ISR) 4–6 6–2 6–1

Great Britain defeated India 3–2, Nottingham GBR
Greg Rusedski (GBR) d. Leander Paes (IND) 2–6 6–3 3–6 6–2 11–9
Tim Henman (GBR) d. Mahesh Bhupathi (IND) 4–6 6–3 6–3 6–3
Mahesh Bhupathi/Leander Paes (IND) d. Neil Broad/Tim Henman (GBR) 7–6(2) 6–3 7–6(3)
Tim Henman (GBR) d. Leander Paes (IND) 7–6(3) 6–2 7–6(5)
Mahesh Bhupathi (IND) d. Chris Wilkinson (GBR) 6–3 6–4

Netherlands defeated Ecuador 5–0, Eindhoven NED
Jan Siemerink (NED) d. Luis Morejon (ECU) 6–3 6–3 6–1
Paul Haarhuis (NED) d. Nicolas Lapentti (ECU) 6–2 6–3 6–2
Jacco Eltingh/Paul Haarhuis (NED) d. Andres Gomez/Nicolas Lapentti (ECU) 5–7 6–1 6–3 6–7(1) 6–4
Jan Siemerink (NED) d. Giovanni Lapentti (ECU) 6–2 6–1
Sjeng Schalken (NED) d. Luis Morejon (ECU) 6–0 6–3

Russia defeated Japan 3–1, Osaka JPN
Yevgeny Kafelnikov (RUS) d. Gouichi Motomura (JPN) 4–6 6–2 6–3 6–3
Marat Safin (RUS) d. Takao Suzuki (JPN) 7–6(4) 6–2 6–3
Yevgeny Kafelnikov/Marat Safin (RUS) d. Gouichi Motomura/Takao Suzuki (JPN) 7–5 6–3 4–6 6–2
Takao Suzuki (JPN) d. Kirill Ivanov Smolensky (RUS) 6–4 6–4
Gouichi Motomura (JPN) led Alexander Volkov (RUS) 6–3 - abandoned due to rain
Slovak Republic defeated Argentina 3–2, Buenos Aires ARG
Dominik Hrbaty (SVK) d. Franco Squillari (ARG) 6–3 6–2 6–2
Hernan Gumy (ARG) d. Karol Kucera (SVK) 6–1 6–1 6–4
Lucas Arnold/Luis Lobo (ARG) d. Dominik Hrbaty/Karol Kucera (SVK) 6–3 6–4 6–4
Karol Kucera (SVK) d. Franco Squillari (ARG) 6–3 6–3 3–6 6–7(3) 6–4
Dominik Hrbaty (SVK) d. Hernan Gumy (ARG) 6–2 3–6 6–4 6–2

Group I

Euro/African Zone

FIRST ROUND
13–15 February

Finland defeated Croatia 3–2, Helsinki FIN
Ville Liukko (FIN) d. Ivan Ljubicic (CRO) 4–6 6–4 7–5 6–4
Sasa Hirszon (CRO) d. Tuomas Ketola (FIN) 6–4 3–6 6–0 7–6(5)
Tuomas Ketola/Ville Liukko (FIN) d. Sasa Hirszon/Ivan Ljubicic (CRO) 6–2 3–6 4–6 6–3 6–4
Tuomas Ketola (FIN) d. Ivan Ljubicic (CRO) 6–3 6–3 6–3
Zelijko Krajan (CRO) d. Ville Liukko (FIN) 7–5 7–6(3)
Ukraine defeated Denmark 3–2, Kiev UKR
Andrei Medvedev (UKR) d. Frederik Fetterlein (DEN) 6–3 6–4 7–5
Kenneth Carlsen (DEN) d. Andrei Rybalko (UKR) 2–6 7–6(4) 6–3
Andrei Medvedev/Dimitri Poliakov (UKR) d. Kenneth Carlsen/Frederik Fetterlein (DEN) 6–3 3–6 6–7(4) 7–6(6) 6–4
Andrei Medvedev (UKR) d. Kenneth Carlsen (DEN) 6–3 6–3 6–3
Frederik Fetterlein (DEN) d. Denis Yakimenko (UKR) 6–2 6–2

SECOND ROUND
3–5 April

France defeated Finland 4–1, Helsinki FIN
Guillaume Raoux (FRA) d. Tuomas Ketola (FIN) 6–1 6–1 6–1
Cedric Pioline (FRA) d. Ville Liukko (FIN) 6–3 7–5 7–5
Nicolas Escude/Guillaume Raoux (FRA) d. Tuomas Ketola/Tommi Lenho (FIN) 7–5 4–6 7–6(1) 6–2
Jerome Golmard (FRA) d. Tapio Nurminen (FIN) 7–6(4) 6–4
Tommi Lenho (FIN) d. Guillaume Raoux (FRA) 6–3 6–4
Romania defeated Norway 4–1, Bucharest ROM
Dinu Pescariu (ROM) d. Jan Frode Andersen (NOR) 7–6(2) 6–4 6–4
Andrei Pavel (ROM) d. Christian Ruud (NOR) 6–2 6–2 6–2
Andrei Pavel/Gabriel Trifu (ROM) d. Lars Hjarrand/Helge Koll (NOR) 6–3 6–2 6–2
Christian Ruud (NOR) d. Dinu Pescariu (ROM) 6–4 4–6 6–4
Andrei Pavel (ROM) d. Jan Frode Andersen (NOR) 6–4 6–4
Israel defeated Austria 4–1, Ramat Hasharon ISR
Eyal Erlich (ISR) d. Gerald Mandl (AUT) 6–1 7–6(4) 7–5
Amir Hadad (ISR) d. Stefan Koubek (AUT) 7–6(5) 6–4 6–3
Noam Behr/Eyal Erlich (ISR) d. Thomas Buchmayer/Wolfgang Schranz (AUT) 6–4 7–6(3) 4–6 1–6 6–4
Noam Behr (ISR) d. Stefan Koubek (AUT) 7–6(3) 6–1
Wolfgang Schranz (AUT) d. Amir Hadad (ISR) 6–4 5–7 6–3
Great Britain defeated Ukraine 5–0, Newcastle GBR
Greg Rusedski (GBR) d. Andrei Rybalko (UKR) 6–4 6–0 6–4
Tim Henman (GBR) d. Andrei Medvedev (UKR) 6–2 6–7(4) 6–4 1–6 6–1
Tim Henman/Greg Rusedski (GBR) d. Andrei Medvedev/Andrei Rybalko (UKR) 6–4 7–5 7–6(9)
Greg Rusedski (GBR) d. Andrei Medvedev (UKR) 6–1 6–4
Tim Henman (GBR) d. Andrei Rybalko (UKR) 6–1 2–6 6–2

PLAYOFF ROUND
25–27 September

Croatia defeated Norway 3–2, Oslo NOR
Christian Ruud (NOR) d. Lovro Zovko (CRO) 7–6(5) 6–4 6–1
Ivan Ljubicic (CRO) d. Jan Frode Andersen (NOR) 6–4 6–4 6–7(5) 6–4
Ivan Ljubicic/Lovro Zovko (CRO) d. Jan Frode Andersen/Christian Ruud (NOR) 6–4 3–6 6–2 3–6 8–6
Ivan Ljubicic (CRO) d. Christian Ruud (NOR) 6–1 6–1 6–3
Jan Frode Andersen (NOR) d. Lovro Zovko (CRO) 6–2 6–3

Austria defeated Denmark 5–0, Portschach AUT
Markus Hipfl (AUT) d. Kenneth Carlsen (DEN) 6–4 6–0 6–3
Stefan Koubek (AUT) d. Thomas Larsen (DEN) 3–6 3–6 6–4 6–0 6–2
Wolfgang Schranz/Thomas Strengberger (AUT) d. Kenneth Carlsen/Frederik Fetterlein (DEN) 6–3 6–2 6–4
Wolfgang Schranz (AUT) d. Frederik Fetterlein (DEN) 6–3 6–7(3) 6–1
Markus Hipfl (AUT) d. Thomas Larsen (DEN) 6–1 6–3

American Zone

FIRST ROUND
13–15 February

Argentina defeated Colombia 5–0, Buenos Aires ARG
Lucas Arnold (ARG) d. Mario Rincon (COL) 6–0 6–2 6–2
Franco Squillari (ARG) d. Miguel Tobon (COL) 6–2 6–1 6–1
Lucas Arnold/Luis Lobo (ARG) d. Mario Rincon/Miguel Tobon (COL) 6–2 7–5 6–1
Franco Squillari (ARG) d. Philippe Moggio (COL) 6–1 6–4
Guillermo Canas (ARG) d. Eduardo Rincon (COL) 6–2 7–6(5)
Ecuador defeated Bahamas 5–0, Nassau BAH
Luis Morejon (ECU) d. Mark Knowles (BAH) 6–4 6–0 6–0
Nicolas Lapentti (ECU) d. Roger Smith (BAH) 6–1 6–2 6–2
Andres Gomez/Nicolas Lapentti (ECU) d. John Farrington/Roger Smith (BAH) 6–4 6–0 6–4
Giovanni Lapentti (ECU) d. Bjorn Munroe (BAH) 6–3 7–6(2)
Luis Morejon (ECU) d. John Farrington (BAH) 6–2 6–1
Canada defeated Mexico 3–2, Halifax N.S. CAN
Alejandro Hernandez (MEX) d. Sebastien Lareau (CAN) 4–6 7–6(4) 6–2 6–1
Daniel Nestor (CAN) d. Luis Herrera (MEX) 6–4 6–7(5) 1–6 6–4 6–3
Sebastien Lareau/Daniel Nestor (CAN) d. Alejandro Hernandez/David Roditi (MEX) 6–1 6–2 6–4
Alejandro Hernandez (MEX) d. Bobby Kokavec (CAN) 6–2 6–0 6–4
Sebastien Lareau (CAN) d. Luis Herrera (MEX) 6–4 6–3 6–3

SECOND ROUND
3–5 April

Argentina defeated Chile 4–1, Buenos Aires ARG
Marcelo Rios (CHI) d. Hernan Gumy (ARG) 6–4 3–6 6–3 7–5
Franco Squillari (ARG) d. Hermes Gamonal (CHI) 6–2 6–4 6–2
Lucas Arnold/Luis Lobo (ARG) d. Nicolas Massu/Marcelo Rios (CHI) 7–5 6–3 6–3
Franco Squillari (ARG) d. Fernando Gonzalez (CHI) 6–3 4–6 6–2 6–0
Hernan Gumy (ARG) d. Hermes Gamonal (CHI) 7–5 6–1
Ecuador defeated Canada 3–2, Guayaquil ECU
Nicolas Lapentti (ECU) d. Sebastien Lareau (CAN) 6–2 6–3 0–6 6–3
Luis Morejon (ECU) d. Daniel Nestor (CAN) 6–2 3–6 7–5 6–2
Sebastien Lareau/Daniel Nestor (CAN) d. Andres Gomez/Nicolas Lapentti (ECU) 4–6 6–4 6–2 6–3
Nicolas Lapentti (ECU) d. Daniel Nestor (CAN) 6–1 7–5 6–2
Jocelyn Robichaud (CAN) d. Giovanni Lapentti (ECU) 6–3 7–6(2)

SECOND PLAYOFF ROUND
17–19 July

Chile defeated Columbia 5–0, Santiago CHI
Marcelo Rios (CHI) d. Philippe Moggio (COL) 6–3 6–0 6–2
Nicolas Massu (CHI) d. Miguel Tobon (COL) 6–2 6–4 6–2
Fernando Gonzalez/Nicolas Massu (CHI) d. Philippe Moggio/Miguel Tobon (COL) 6–7(7) 7–5 7–6(6) 6–4
Marcelo Rios (CHI) d. Miguel Tobon (COL) 6–2 6–2
Nicolas Massu (CHI) d. Jaime Cortes (COL) 6–1 2–0 ret.
Bahamas defeated Mexico 3–2, Guadalajara MEX
Mark Knowles (BAH) d. Luis Herrera (MEX) 6–3 1–6 6–2 6–2
Alejandro Hernandez (MEX) d. Roger Smith (BAH) 6–3 6–1 6–3
Mark Knowles/Roger Smith (BAH) d. David Roditi/Mariano Sanchez (MEX) 7–5 7–6(5) 7–5
Mark Knowles (BAH) d. Alejandro Hernandez (MEX) 4–6 6–3 1–6 6–2 6–1
Mariano Sanchez (MEX) d. Dentry Mortimer (BAH) 6–2 6–0

THIRD PLAYOFF ROUND
25–27 September

Colombia defeated Mexico 3–2, Cali COL
Alejandro Hernandez (MEX) d. Miguel Tobon (COL) 7–6(4) 6–3 6–3
Mauricio Hadad (COL) d. Mariano Sanchez (MEX) 5–7 6–3 6–3 6–4
Mauricio Hadad/Miguel Tobon (COL) d. Marco Osorio/David Roditi (MEX) 7–6(3) 6–4 5–7 6–7(5) 7–5
Mauricio Hadad (COL) d. Alejandro Hernandez (MEX) 6–4 6–3 6–1
Mariano Sanchez (MEX) d. Miguel Tobon (COL) 3–6 6–1 7–5

Asia/Oceania Zone

FIRST ROUND
13–15 February

Uzbekistan defeated China P.R. 5–0, Tashkent UZB
Vadim Kutsenko (UZB) d. Yue-Wei Wang (CHN) 6–2 6–2 6–1
Oleg Ogorodov (UZB) d. Yu Zhang (CHN) 6–3 3–6 6–1 6–4
Oleg Ogorodov/Dmitri Tomashevich (UZB) d. Ling Lu/Yu Zhang (CHN) 3–6 7–6(6) 6–4 6–4
Oleg Ogorodov (UZB) d. Lu Zheng (CHN) 6–4 6–4
Vadim Kutsenko (UZB) d. Yu Zhang (CHN) 6–3 3–6 6–0

Japan defeated Indonesia 5–0, Sapporo JPN
Takao Suzuki (JPN) d. Andrian Raturandang (INA) 6–1 6–4 6–4
Gouichi Motomura (JPN) d. Dede Suhendar Dinata (INA) 6–1 6–3 6–2
Satochi Iwabuchi/Takao Suzuki (JPN) d. Andrian Raturandang/Sulistyo Wibowo (INA) 6–4 7–6(6) 6–3
Gouichi Motomura (JPN) d. Andrian Raturandang (INA) 6–3 6–2
Takao Suzuki (JPN) d. Dede Suhendar Dinata (INA) 6–3 6–4

New Zealand defeated Lebanon 3–2, Beirut LIB
Alistair Hunt (NZL) d. Ali Hamadeh (LIB) 6–4 6–4 6–4
Jicham Zaatini (LIB) d. James Greenhalgh (NZL) 6–4 6–2 7–5
James Greenhalgh/Alistair Hunt (NZL) d. Ali Hamadeh/Jicham Zaatini (LIB) 6–3 6–4 6–2
Alistair Hunt (NZL) d. Jicham Zaatini (LIB) 7–5 7–6(4) 7–6(8)
Ali Hamadeh (LIB) d. James Greenhalgh (NZL) 6–3 6–4

SECOND ROUND
3–5 April

Japan defeated New Zealand 3–2, Miyazaki City JPN
Gouichi Motomura (JPN) d. Teo Susnjak (NZL) 6–0 6–0 6–0
Takao Suzuki (JPN) d. Brett Steven (NZL) 7–6(4) 7–6(5) 7–5
James Greenhalgh/Brett Steven (NZL) d. Satoshi Iwabuchi/Takao Suzuki (JPN) 4–6 6–3 6–4 6–3
Brett Steven (NZL) d. Gouichi Motomura (JPN) 3–6 6–2 3–6 6–3 6–4
Takao Suzuki (JPN) d. Teo Susnjak (NZL) 6–4 6–7(5) 6–4 6–1

Uzbekistan defeated Korea 3–1, Seoul KOR
Vadim Kutsenko (UZB) d. Yong-il Yoon (KOR) 4–6 6–4 6–4 6–2
Hyung-Taik Lee (KOR) d. Oleg Ogorodov (UZB) 7–5 6–2 6–4
Oleg Ogorodov/Dmitri Tomashevich (UZB) d. Dong-Hyun Kim/Hyung-Taik Lee (KOR) 6–2 4–6 6–3 7–6(2)
Oleg Ogorodov (UZB) d. Yong-il Yoon (KOR) 6–4 6–7(4) 6–4 7–6(2)
Yung-Taik Lee (KOR) vs. Vadim Kutsenko (UZB) - not played

SECOND ROUND PLAYOFFS
17–19 July

Korea defeated China 4–1, Seoul KOR
Yong-Il Yoon (KOR) d. Jing-Zhu Yang (CHN) 6–3 6–2 6–0
Hyung-Taik Lee (KOR) d. Yu-Wei Wang (CHN) 6–1 6–2 6–0
Dong-Hyun Kim/Nam-Hoon Kim (KOR) d. Ling Lu/Jing-Zhu Yang (CHN) 6–1 3–6 6–2 3–6 6–2
Yu-Wei Wang (CHN) d. Yong-Il Yoon (KOR) 2–6 6–3 7–6(1)
Hyung-Taik Lee (KOR) d. Ling Lu (CHN) 6–4 6–3

Lebanon defeated Indonesia 3–2, Beirut LIB
Ali Hamadeh (LIB) d. Andrian Raturandang (INA) 7–6(6) 6–3 7–6(5)
Jicham Zaatini (LIB) d. Feby Widianto (INA) 6–4 3–6 6–3 6–4
Ali Hamadeh/Jicham Zaatini (LIB) d. Sulistyo Wibowo/Bonit Wiryawan (INA) 7–6(4) 6–4 6–4
Andrian Raturandang (INA) d. Sean Karam (LIB) 6–2 4–6 6–2
Feby Widianto (INA) d. Alex Zakharia (LIB) 6–3 7–5

THIRD ROUND PLAYOFF
25–27 September

China defeated Indonesia 5–0, Yanji City CHN
Yu Zhang (CHN) d. Feby Widianto (INA) 6–1 6–2 4–6 1–6 7–5
Yu Zheng (CHN) d. Andrian Raturandang (INA) 6–3 6–2 6–2
Si Li/Yu Zheng (CHN) d. Sulistyo Wibowo/Bonit Wiryawan (INA) 4–6 7–6(7) 6–4 6–3
Yu Zhang (CHN) d. Andrian Raturandang (INA) 3–6 6–3 6–4
Yu Zheng (CHN) d. Feby Widianto (INA) 6–2 6–1

Group II

Euro/African Zone

FIRST ROUND
1–3 May

Morocco defeated Bulgaria 3–2, Meknes MAR
Karim Alami (MAR) d. Milen Velev (BUL) 7–6(3) 4–6 7–6(2) 6–2
Orlin Stanoytchev (BUL) d. Mehdi Tahiri (MAR) 6–2 2–6 6–3 3–6 6–2
Karim Alami/Mounir El Aarej (MAR) d. Orlin Stanoytchev/Milen Velev (BUL) 6–4 7–5 6–2
Karim Alami (MAR) d. Orlin Stanoytchev (BUL) 3–6 6–3 6–7(5) 6–3 6–1
Milen Velev (BUL) d. Mehdi Tahiri (MAR) 6–2 6–3

Belarus defeated Luxembourg 5–0, Minsk BLR
Maxim Mirnyi (BLR) d. Adrian Graimprey (LUX) 7–5 6–4 6–4
Alexander Shvec (BLR) d. Sacha Thoma (LUX) 6–4 6–2 6–4
Maxim Mirnyi/Alexander Shvec (BLR) d. Adrian Graimprey/Sacha Thoma (LUX) 6–3 6–2 6–3
Evgeni Mikheev (BLR) d. Roland Theisen (LUX) 6–3 6–2
Maxim Mirnyi (BLR) d. Sacha Thoma (LUX) 7–5 6–3

Senegal defeated Poland 3–2, Dakar SEN
Jerzy Stasiak (POL) d. Thierno Ly (SEN) 6–3 6–4 6–2
Yahiya Doumbia (SEN) d. Bartlomiej Dabrowski (POL) 6–1 3–6 4–6 7–6(8) 6–3
Yahiya Doumbia/Thierno Ly (SEN) d. Bartlomiej Dabrowski/ Jerzy Stasiak (POL) 6–4 6–7(0) 6–7(4) 6–4 6–4
Yahiya Doumbia (SEN) d. Jerzy Stasiak (POL) 6–2 6–4 3–6 2–6 6–2
Bartlomiej Dabrowski (POL) d. Daouda Senga Ndiaye (SEN) 6–2 6–2

Cote d'Ivoire defeated Egypt 3–2, Abidjan CIV
Claude N'Goran (CIV) d. Amr Ghoneim (EGY) 6–2 6–1 7–5
Gehad El Deeb (EGY) d. Valentin Sanon (CIV) 6–3 3–6 6–2 5–0 ret.
Amr Ghoneim/Karim Maamoun (EGY) d. Claude N'Goran/Nouhoun Sangare (CIV) 7–6(2) 7–6(4) 6–3
Nouhon Sangare (CIV) d. Amr Ghoneim (EGY) 6–7(4) 6–3 6–4 4–6 8–6
Claude N'Goran (CIV) d. Gehad El Deeb (EGY) 6–1 6–4 6–1

Yugoslavia defeated Latvia 3–2, Jurmala LAT
Andris Filimonovs (LAT) d. Dusan Vemic (YUG) 6–7(7) 7–6(5) 6–4 6–4
Nenad Zimonjic (YUG) d. Girts Dzelde (LAT) 6–0 4–6 6–4 7–5
Dusan Vemic/Nenad Zimonjic (YUG) d. Girts Dzelde/Nils Ivanovs (LAT) 6–4 6–3 6–1
Girts Dzelde (LAT) d. Dusan Vemic (YUG) 6–4 6–3 6–7(8) 1–6 6–2
Nenad Zimonjic (YUG) d. Andris Filimonovs (LAT) 6–3 6–4 6–2

Portugal defeated Georgia 5–0, Braga POR
Nuno Marques (POR) d. Irakli Kunchulia (GEO) 6–0 6–3 6–2
Joao Cunha-Silva (POR) d. Vladimir Margalitadze (GEO) 6–2 6–3 6–3
Emanuel Couto/Bernardo Mota (POR) d. Vladimir Margalitadze/Givi Samkharadze (GEO) 7–6(3) 6–1 6–3
Nuno Marques (POR) d. Vladimir Margalitadze (GEO) 7–5 6–3
Joao Cunha-Silva (POR) d. Givi Samkaradze (GEO) 6–0 6–3

Slovenia defeated Monaco 5–0, Monte Carlo MON
Iztok Bozic (SLO) d. Christophe Bosio (MON) 6–3 6–2 6–2
Borut Urh (SLO) d. Sebastien Graeff (MON) 6–1 6–2 6–3
Andrej Krasevec/Borut Urh (SLO) d. Christophe Bosio/Sebastien Graeff (MON) 6–4 4–6 6–1 6–3
Marc Tkalec (SLO) d. Sebastien Graeff (MON) 6–4 6–2
Andrei Krasevec (SLO) d. Christophe Bosio (MON) 3–6 6–4 6–2

Hungary defeated Ireland 4–1, Budapest HUN
Norbert Mazany (HUN) d. Scott Barron (IRL) 6–4 0–6 2–6 6–3 9–7
Attila Savolt (HUN) d. John Doran (IRL) 6–1 6–3 6–3
Kornel Bardoczky/Attila Savolt (HUN) d. Owen Casey/Tom Hamilton (IRL) 6–3 6–4 1–6 6–1
Attila Savolt (HUN) d. Scott Barron (IRL) 6–4 6–2
John Doran (IRL) d. Norbert Mazany (HUN) 6–3 3–6 6–3

SECOND ROUND
17–19 July

Belarus defeated Morocco 3–2, Agadir MAR
Hicham Arazi (MAR) d. Alexander Shvec (BLR) 6–3 4–6 7–5 6–4
Vladimir Voltchkov (BLR) d. Mounir El Aarej (MAR) 2–6 6–3 6–2 6–4
Maxim Mirnyi/Vladimir Voltchkov (BLR) d. Hicham Arazi/Mounir El Aarej (MAR) 6–7(3) 6–7(5) 7–6(3) 6–3 6–4
Hicham Arazi (MAR) d. Vladimir Voltchkov (BLR) 2–6 6–7(4) 6–3 6–4 6–4
Alexander Shvec (BLR) d. Mounir El Aarej (MAR) 5–7 6–2 3–6 6–4 7–5

Cote d'Ivoire defeated Senegal 3–2, Dakar SEN
Valentin Sanon (CIV) d. Jean Noel Said (SEN) 6–1 6–1 6–0
Yahiya Doumbia (SEN) d. Claude N'Goran (CIV) 6–4 6–4 6–7(2) 4–6 6–4
Ilou Lonfo/Claude N'Goran (CIV) d. Yahiya Doumbia/Thierno Ly (SEN) 6–4 6–7(9) 6–3 7–6(4)
Yahiya Doumbia (SEN) d. Valentin Sanon (CIV) 6–2 6–4 6–3
Claude N'Goran (CIV) d. Thierno Ly (SEN) 6–1 6–4 6–1

Portugal defeated Yugoslavia 3–2, Belgrade YUG
Dusan Vemic (YUG) d. Joao Cunha-Silva (POR) 7–6(3) 6–3 1–6 6–3
Nuno Marques (POR) d. Nenad Zimonjic (YUG) 3–6 6–0 2–6 6–3 20–18
Emanuel Couto/Joao Cunha-Silva (POR) d. Nebojsa Djordjevic/Dusan Vemic (YUG) 6–7(5) 4–6 7–6(2) 6–2 6–3
Dusan Vemic (YUG) d. Nuno Marques (POR) 3–6 7–6(7) 6–3 6–3
Joao Cunha-Silva (POR) d. Nenad Zimonjic (YUG) 0–6 6–7(2) 6–3 7–5 6–1

Hungary defeated Slovenia 3–2, Budapest HUN
Attila Savolt (HUN) d. Borut Urh (SLO) 6–2 6–4 6–3
Kornel Bardoczky (HUN) d. Iztok Bozic (SLO) 6–0 6–3 1–6 6–4
Gabor Koves/Attila Savolt (HUN) d. Iztok Bozic/Andrej Kracman (SLO) 6–4 7–5 6–2
Marko Tkalec (SLO) d. Attila Savolt (HUN) 7–5 6–4
Andrej Kracman (SLO) d. Kornel Bardoczky (HUN) 4–6 7–5 6–3

THIRD ROUND
25–27 September

Belarus defeated Cote d'Ivoire 4–1, Abidjan CIV
Maxim Mirnyi (BLR) d. Valentin Sanon (CIV) 6–1 7–6(4) 7–6(6)
Vladimir Voltchkov (BLR) d. Claude N'Goran (CIV) 7–5 7–6(6) 7–6(6)
Maxim Mirnyi/Vladimir Voltchkov (BLR) d. Ilou Lonfo/Claude N'Goran (CIV) 6–3 6–7(3) 6–3 4–6 7–5
Alexander Shvec (BLR) d. Valentin Sanon (CIV) 7–5 6–4
Claude N'Goran (CIV) d. Evgeni Mikheev (BLR) 6–4 6–1

Portugal defeated Hungary 4–1, Albufeira POR
Nuno Marques (POR) d. Gergely Kisgyorgy (HUN) 5–7 7–6(4) 6–0 6–3
Joao Cunha-Silva (POR) d. Attila Savolt (HUN) 6–1 6–4 6–3
Emanuel Couto/Nuno Marques (POR) d. Gabor Koves/Attila Savolt (HUN) 0–6 7–6(4) 6–3 2–6 9–7
Nuno Marques (POR) d. Balazs Veress (HUN) 6–3 6–3
Gergely Kisgyorgy (HUN) d. Andre Lopes (POR) 6–3 3–6 6–2

SECOND ROUND PLAYOFF
17–19 July

Ireland defeated Monaco 5–0, Dublin IRL
John Doran (IRL) d. Christophe Bosio (MON) 6–3 6–3 6–1
Owen Casey (IRL) d. Sebastien Graeff (MON) 6–2 6–3 6–1
Owen Casey/Tom Hamilton (IRL) d. Christophe Boggetti/Sebastien Graeff (MON) 7–6(2) 6–4 6–1
George McGill (IRL) d. Christophe Bosio (MON) 6–3 3–6 7–5
John Doran (IRL) d. Sebastien Graeff (MON) 7–6(1) 6–7(6) 7–6(5)

Latvia defeated Georgia 5–0, Jurmala LAT
Girts Dzelde (LAT) d. Givi Samkharadze (GEO) 6–3 4–6 6–3 6–0
Andris Filimonovs (LAT) d. Irakli Kunchulia (GEO) 6–2 6–3 3–6 6–3
Girts Dzelde/Andris Filimonovs (LAT) d. David Katcharava/Givi Samkharadze (GEO) 6–1 6–3 6–3
Andris Filimonovs (LAT) d. Givi Samkharadze (GEO) 6–3 6–2
Girts Dzelde (LAT) d. Irakli Kunchulia (GEO) 6–3 6–1

Poland defeated Egypt 4–1, Bydgoszcz POL
Bartlomiej Dabrowski (POL) d. Tamer El Sawy (EGY) 6–2 6–3 6–3
Michal Chmela (POL) d. Amr Ghoneim (EGY) 6–1 6–1 6–4
Michal Chmela/Bartlomiej Dabrowski (POL) d. Tamer El Sawy/Hisham Hemeda (EGY) 6–0 7–6(2) 6–3
Jerzy Stasiak (POL) d. Karim Maamoun (EGY) 5–7 6–2 6–3
Amr Ghoneim (EGY) d. Piotr Szczepanik (POL) 6–4 6–4

Bulgaria defeated Luxembourg 5–0, Sofia BUL
Milen Velev (BUL) d. Pascal Schaul (LUX) 6–3 6–1 7–5
Orlin Stanoytchev (BUL) d. Mike Scheidweiler (LUX) 6–2 6–2 6–1
Orlin Stanoytchev/Milen Velev (BUL) d. Adrian Graimprey/Pascal Schaul (LUX) 6–3 6–2 6–4
Ivailo Traykov (BUL) d. Pascal Schaul (LUX) 6–3 6–1
Ivo Bratanov (BUL) d. Mike Scheidweiler (LUX) 5–7 6–2 6–2

American Zone

FIRST ROUND
3–5 April

Venezuela defeated Guatemala 4–1, Caracas VEN
Jimy Szymanski (VEN) d. Luiz Perez-Chete (GUA) 6–0 6–3 6–4
Kepler Orellana (VEN) d. Jacobo Chavez (GUA) 6–3 6–3 6–4
Kepler Orellana/Jimy Szymanski (VEN) d. Daniel Chavez/Luis Valencia (VEN) 6–4 6–2 6–2
Jose de Armas (VEN) d. Jacobo Chavez (GUA) 6–2 6–4
Luis Perez-Chete (GUA) d. Ricardo Omana (VEN) 7–6(4) 6–4

Haiti defeated Cuba 3–2, Port-au-Prince HAI
Ronald Agenor (HAI) d. Armando Perez (CUB) 6–2 6–2 6–0
Lazaro Navarro (CUB) d. Bertrand Madsen (HAI) 6–5 6–7(4) 6–4 4–6 6–3
Lazaro Navarro/Juan Pino (CUB) d. Ronald Agenor/Jerry Joseph (HAI) 6–4 6–3 2–6 6–4
Ronald Agenor (HAI) d. Lazaro Navarro (CUB) 6–2 6–1 6–4
Bertrand Madsen (HAI) d. Armando Perez (CUB) 6–3 4–6 6–2 6–2

Peru defeated Jamaica 5–0, Lima PER
Luis Horna (PER) d. Jermaine Smith (JAM) 6–1 6–2 7–6(6)
Alejandro Aramburu (PER) d. Karl Hale (JAM) 6–4 6–2 3–6 6–3
Luis Horna/Americo Venero (PER) d. Karl Hale/Nicholas Malcolm (JAM) 6–1 6–3 6–3
Alejandro Aramburu (PER) d. Jermaine Smith (JAM) 6–1 6–4
Ivan Miranda (PER) d. Jessi Smatt (JAM) 6–3 6–1

Uruguay defeated Paraguay 3–2, Montevideo URU
Ramon Delgado (PAR) d. Federico Dondo (URU) 6–0 6–3 6–1
Marcelo Filippini (URU) d. Ricardo Mena (PAR) 6–2 6–1 4–6 6–1
Marcelo Filippini/Gonzalo Rodriguez (URU) d. Ramon Delgado/Ricardo Mena (PAR) 6–3 6–3 1–6 7–6(6)
Ramon Delgado (PAR) d. Marcelo Filippini (URU) 7–5 3–6 7–5 6–7(2) 6–2
Federico Dondo (URU) d. Ricardo Mena (PAR) 6–7(6) 6–4 6–2 7–6(6)

SECOND ROUND
17–19 July

Venezuela defeated Haiti 3–2, Port-au-Prince HAI
Ronald Agenor (HAI) d. Keppler Orellana (VEN) 6–2 6–3 7–5
Jimy Szymanski (VEN) d. Bertrand Madsen (HAI) 6–4 6–4 6–1
Keppler Orellana/Jimy Szymanski (VEN) d. Ronald Agenor/Bertrand Madsen (HAI) 6–3 6–4 4–6 6–4
Ronald Agenor (HAI) d. Jimy Szymanski (VEN) 7–5 7–6(4) 3–6 6–0
Keppler Orellana (VEN) d. Bertrand Madsen (HAI) 6–1 6–2 6–2

Uruguay defeated Peru 4–1, Montevideo URU
Marcelo Filippini (URU) d. Americo Venero (PER) 6–7(1) 7–5 6–3 6–0
Federico Dondo (URU) d. Alejandro Aramburu (PER) 6–4 6–1 7–5
Marcelo Filippini/Gonzalo Rodriguez (URU) d. Ivan Miranda/Americo Venero (PER) 6–3 7–5 6–3
Alejandro Aramburu (PER) d. Alberto Brause (URU) 6–3 ret.
Federico Dondo (URU) d. Americo Venero (PER) 6–2 6–4

FINAL ROUND
25–27 September

Venezuela defeated Uruguay 3–2, Montevideo URU
Marcelo Filippini (URU) d. Kepler Orellana (VEN) 6–2 6–3 7–5
Jimy Szymanski (VEN) d. Federico Dondo (URU) 2–6 7–5 6–4 6–1
Kepler Orellana/Jimy Szymanski (VEN) d. Marcelo Filippini/Gonzalo Rodriguez (URU) 2–6 2–6 6–2 6–2 6–4
Marcelo Filippini (URU) d. Jimy Szymanski (VEN) 6–3 6–7(2) 6–3 6–3
Kepler Orellana (VEN) d. Federico Dondo (URU) 4–6 6–2 3–6 6–4 6–1

PLAYOFF ROUND
17–19 July

Cuba defeated Guatemala 3–2, Havana CUB
Lazaro Navarro (CUB) d. Alexander Lehnhoff (GUA) 6–1 6–4 6–2
Juan Antonio Pino (CUB) d. Jacobo Chavez (GUA) 6–3 6–3 6–7(5) 1–6 7–5
Lazaro Navarro/Juan Antonio Pino (CUB) d. Daniel Chavez/Luis Valencia (GUA) 6–4 6–4 6–4
Daniel Chavez (GUA) d. Jorge Catala (CUB) 7–6(5) 6–2
Alexander Lehnhoff (GUA) d. Sandor Martinez (CUB) 6–3 6–7(7) 6–1

Paraguay defeated Jamaica 5–0, Asuncion PAR
Ricardo Mena (PAR) d. Jermaine Smith (JAM) 6–3 6–4 6–4
Ramon Delgado (PAR) d. Karl Hale (JAM) 6–0 6–4 6–2
Ramon Delgado/Ricardo Mena (PAR) d. Karl Hale/Jermaine Smith (JAM) 3–6 6–2 6–2 6–1
Ramon Delgado (PAR) d. Jermaine Smith (JAM) 6–0 6–2
Francisco Rodriguez (PAR) d. Jessie Smatt (JAM) 6–3 6–1

Asia/Oceania Zone

FIRST ROUND
3–5 April

Thailand defeated Philippines 4–1, Manila PHI
Paradorn Srichaphan (THA) d. Adelo Abadia (PHI) 6–1 6–4 1–6 4–6 7–5
Joseph Lizardo (PHI) d. Narathorn Srichaphan (THA) 3–6 6–2 3–6 7–6(2) 6–4
Wittaya Samrej/Danai Udomchoke (THA) d. Robert Angelo/Bryan Juinio (PHI) 1–6 6–4 6–4 6–4
Paradorn Srichaphan (THA) d. Joseph Lizardo (PHI) 6–2 3–6 7–6(5) 6–4
Narathorn Srichaphan (THA) d. Adelo Abadia (PHI) 6–4 2–6 6–4

Chinese Taipei defeated China Hong Kong 3–2, I-Lan City TPE
Chia-Yen Tsai (TPE) d. Christopher Lai (HKG) 6–2 6–3 6–3
Melvin Tong (HKG) d. Chih-Jung Chen (TPE) 2–6 6–1 6–4 2–6 8–6
Chih-Jung Chen/Bing-Chao Lin (TPE) d. Christopher Lai/Stephen So (HKG) 3–6 6–1 6–1
Melvin Tong (HKG) d. Chia-Yen Tsai (TPE) 6–7(4) 6–4 6–1 6–0
Chih-Jung Chen (TPE) d. Christopher Lai (HKG) 6–4 6–2 6–0

Pakistan defeated Pacific Oceania 5–0, Islamabad PAK
Asim Shafik (PAK) d. Lency Tenai (POC) 6–0 6–1 6–0
Mohammad Khaliq (PAK) d. Lawrence Tere (POC) 6–1 7–5 6–1
Mohammad Khaliq/Asam Shafik (PAK) d. Lawrence Tere/Sanjeev Tikaram (POC) 7–5 6–4 6–2
Aqeel Khan (PAK) d. Sanjeev Tikaram (POC) 6–1 6–3
Nasser Shirazi (PAK) d. Lawrence Tere (POC) 6–3 6–4

17–19 April

Iran defeated Qatar 5–0, Tehran IRI
Farhad Tadayon (IRI) d. Mohamed Ali Haji (QAT) 6–3 6–4 6–0
Farshad Talavar (IRI) d. Mubarak Al-Tubaishi (QAT) 6–2 4–6 6–0 6–0
Ramin Raziani/Akbar Taheri (IRI) d. Mohamed Ali Haji/Mohamed Al-Saoud (QAT) 6–3 6–2 6–2
Farshad Talavar (IRI) d. Mohamed Ali Haji (QAT) 6–1 6–2
Farhad Tadayon (IRI) d. Mubarak Al-Tubaishi (QAT) 6–2 6–3

SECOND ROUND
17–19 July

Thailand defeated Chinese Taipei 3–2, Pattaya City THA
Paradorn Srichaphan (THA) d. Chih-Jung Chen (TPE) 6–4 6–4 6–2
Wei-Ju Chen (TPE) d. Narathorn Srichaphan (THA) 6–1 7–6(4) 6–1
Wittaya Samrej/Narathorn Srichaphan (THA) d. Chih-Jung Chen/Bing-Chao Lin (TPE)
7–6(6) 3–6 6–3 6–3
Paradorn Srichaphan (THA) d. Wei-Ju Chen (TPE) 6–2 6–3 4–6 2–6 6–1
Chia-Yen Tsai (TPE) d. Narathorn Srichaphan (THA) 7–6(6) 6–2
Pakistan defeated Iran 4–1, Tehran IRI
Mohammad Khaliq (PAK) d. Farhad Tadayon (IRI) 6–3 6–3 7–6(2)
Asim Shafik (PAK) d. Akbar Taheri (IRI) 6–4 6–4 6–4
Mohammad Khaliq/Asim Shafik (PAK) d. Farhad Tadayon/Akbar Taheri (IRI) 6–1 6–4 6–4
Aqeel Khan (PAK) d. Farshad Talavar (IRI) 4–6 6–1 6–4
Shahab-Nafez Hassani (IRI) d. Nasir Sherazi (PAK) 6–3 6–2

FINAL ROUND
25–27 September

Pakistan defeated Thailand 3–2, Lahore PAK
Aisam Qureshi (PAK) d. Danai Udomchoke (THA) 6–3 6–3 6–3
Paradorn Srichaphan (THA) d. Mohammad Khaliq (PAK) 6–3 6–4 1–6 6–7(6) 10–8
Mohammad Khaliq/Aisam Qureshi (PAK) d. Wittaya Samrej/Narathorn Srichaphan (THA)
6–4 6–3 6–1
Paradorn Srichaphan (THA) d. Aisam Qureshi (PAK) 6–7(5) 7–6(1) 4–6 7–5 12–10
Mohammad Khaliq (PAK) d. Narathorn Srichaphan (THA) 4–6 6–1 6–3 6–2

PLAYOFF ROUND
17–19 July

Philippines defeated China Hong Kong 4–1, Causeway Bay HKG
Joseph Lizardo (PHI) d. John Hui (HKG) 7–6(5) 3–6 3–2 ret.
Bryan Juinio (PHI) d. Melvin Tong (HKG) 6–2 4–6 6–3 6–3
Adelo Abadia/Michael John Misa (PHI) d. Shane Barr/Andrew Brothers (HKG) 7–5 7–5 6–4
Melvin Tong (HKG) d. Joseph Lizardo (PHI) 7–5 6–4
Bryan Juinio (PHI) d. Shane Barr (HKG) 6–2 6–2
Qatar defeated Pacific Oceania 4–1, Doha QAT
Nasser Al-Khulaifi (QAT) d. Lency Tenai (POC) 6–7(4) 6–4 6–4 6–2
Sultan Al-Alawi (QAT) d. Lawrence Tere (POC) 6–4 6–0 6–2
Lency Tenai/Lawrence Tere (POC) d. Sultan Al-Alawi/Nasser Al-Khulaifi (QAT) 6–7(5) 6–3
4–6 7–6(2) 8–6
Sultan Al-Alawi (QAT) d. Lency Tenai (POC) 6–3 6–1 6–2
Nasser Al-Khulaifi (QAT) d. Lawrence Tere (POC) 7–5 6–2

Group III

Euro/African Zone A
21–25 January, Lome, Togo

GROUP A

Ghana defeated Madagascar 2–1
Isaac Donkor (GHA) d. Harivony Andrianafetra (MAD) 6–3 6–3
Frank Ofori (GHA) d. Andriamirija Rajoabelina (MAD) 4–6 7–6(5) 6–3
Jean-Marc Randriamanalina/Germain Rasolondrazana (MAD) d. Gunther Darkey/Tetteh
Quaye (GHA) 6–3 7–5
Estonia defeated Cyprus 2–1
Rene Busch (EST) d. Marianos Baghdatis (CYP) 7–5 2–6 6–3
Demetrios Leondis (CYP) d. Alti Vahkal (EST) 7–6(4) 6–3
Andrei Luzgin/Gert Vilms (EST) d. Demetrios Leondis/Neoklis Neokleous (CYP) 6–4 6–4

Ghana defeated Cyprus 3–0
Isaac Donkor (GHA) d. Marinos Baghdatis (CYP) 3–6 7–5 6–3
Frank Ofori (GHA) d. George Kalanov (CYP) 6–2 6–2
Gunther Darkey/Tetteh Quaye (GHA) d. Demetrios Leondis/Neoklis Neokleous (CYP) 6–3 6–0
Estonia defeated Madagascar 2–1
Rene Busch (EST) d. Harivony Andrianafetra (MAD) 1–6 6–4 6–4
Andriamirija Rajoabelina (MAD) d. Andrei Luzgin (EST) 3–6 6–4 6–2
Alti Vahkal/Gert Vilms (EST) d. Harivony Andrianafetra/Andriamirija Rajoabelina(MAD) 7–5 7–5

Estonia defeated Ghana 2–1
Rene Busch (EST) d. Tetteh Quaye (GHA) 5–7 6–2 6–0
Alti Vahkal (EST) d. Gunther Darkey (GHA) 6–3 3–0 ret.
Isaac Donkor/Frank Ofori (GHA) d. Andrei Luzgin/Gert Vilms (EST) 6–1 6–2
Cyprus defeated Madagascar 2–1
Marinos Baghdatis (CYP) d. Germain Rasolondrazana (MAD) 3–6 6–2 6–3
Demetrios Leondis (CYP) d. Jean-Marc Randriamanalina (MAD) 7–6(4) 2–6 6–4
Harivony Andrianafetra/Germain Rasolondrazana (MAD) d. George Kalanov/Neoklis
Neokleous (CYP) 6–3 6–1

GROUP B

Togo defeated Bosnia/Herzegovina 2–1
Komi Loglo (TOG) d. Merid Zahirovic (BIH) 6–4 6–4
Gerard Gbedey (TOG) d. Kristian Capalik (BIH) 6–2 6–2
Haris Basalic/Kristian Capalik (BIH) d. Komi Adeyo/Essenam Loglo (TOG) 6–4 6–3
Kenya defeated Greece 2–1
Allan Cooper (KEN) d. Nikos Rovas (GRE) 3–6 6–3 6–2
Paul Wekesa (KEN) d. Anastassios Vasiliadis (GRE) 6–4 6–4
Nikos Karagiannis/Anastassios Vasiliadis (GRE) d. Allan Cooper/Norbert Oduor (KEN) 6–4 6–3

Togo defeated Greece 3–0
Komi Logo (TOG) d. Nikos Rovas (GRE) 4–6 6–3 6–4
Gerard Gbedey (TOG) d. Anastassios Vasiliadis (GRE) 3–6 6–2 6–1
Essenam Loglo/Komi Loglo (TOG) d. Nikos Karagiannis/Yannis Vlachos (GRE) 6–7(7) 6–1 6–4
Bosnia/Herzegovina defeated Kenya 3–0
Merid Zahirovic (BIH) d. Allan Cooper (KEN) 6–4 6–2
Kristian Capalik (BIH) d. Paul Wekesa (KEN) 6–3 6–3
Haris Basalic/Kristian Capalik (BIH) d. Allan Cooper/Norbert Oduor (KEN) 6–3 6–4.

Greece defeated Bosnia/Herzegovina 3–0
Nikos Rovas (GRE) d. Merid Zahirovic (BIH) 6–1 6–4
Anastassios Vasiliadis (GRE) d. Kristian Capalik (BIH) 6–3 6–2
Nikos Karagiannis/Anastassios Vasiliadis (GRE) d. Haris Basalic/Kristian Capalik (BIH) 6–1 6–4
Togo defeated Kenya 2–1
Komi Loglo (TOG) d. Allan Cooper (KEN) 6–0 6–4
Gerard Gbedey (TOG) d. Paul Wekesa (KEN) 6–7(5) 1–1 ret.
Allan Cooper/Norbert Oduor (KEN) d. Komi Adeyo/Essenam Loglo (TOG) 6–1 7–5

SEMIFINALS

Togo defeated Ghana 3–0
Komi Loglo (TOG) d. Isaac Donkor (GHA) 6–2 7–5
Gerard Gbedey (TOG) d. Frank Ofori (GHA) 6–3 7–6(5)
Komi Adeyo/Essenam Loglo (TOG) d. Gunther Darkey/Tetteh Quaye (GHA) 6–1 4–6 6–3
Greece defeated Estonia 3–0
Nikos Rovas (GRE) d. Alti Vahkal (EST) 7–5 6–2
Anastiassios Vasiliadis (GRE) d. Andrei Luzgin (EST) 6–3 6–4
Nikos Karagiannis/Yannis Vlachos (GRE) d. Rene Busch/Gert Vilms (EST) 6–3 7–5

FINAL

Greece defeated Togo 2–1
Komi Loglo (TOG) d. Nikos Rovas (GRE) 7–6(6) 6–4
Anastassios Vasiliadis (GRE) d. Gerard Gbedey (TOG) 7–6(2) 6–3
Nikos Karagiannis/Anastassios Vasiliadis (GRE) d. Essenam Loglo/Komi Loglo (TOG) 7–6(5) 6–4

PLAYOFF FOR 3RD/4TH POSITIONS

Estonia defeated Ghana 2–1
Andrei Luzgin (EST) d. Tetteh Quaye (GHA) 6–3 6–3
Gunther Darkey (GHA) d. Gert Vilms (EST) 7–5 6–1
Andrei Luzgin/Alti Vahkal (EST) d. Isaac Donkor/Frank Ofori (GHA) 6–7(5) 6–3 7–5

PLAYOFF FOR 5TH–8TH POSITIONS

Bosnia/Herzegovina defeated Madagascar 2–1
Merid Zahirovic (BIH) d. Jean-Marc Randriamanalina (MAD) 6–2 6–1
Kristian Capalik (BIH) d. Andriamirija Rajoabelina (MAD) 6–1 7–5
Harivony Andrianafetra/Andriamirija Rajoabelina (MAD) d. Haris Basalic/Igor Stjepic (BIH)
7–6(3) 6–3
Kenya defeated Cyprus 3–0
Norbert Oduor (KEN) d. Marinos Baghdatis (CYP) 4–6 7–6(2) 6–1
Allan Cooper (KEN) d. Demetrios Leondis (CYP) 6–1 6–1
Barry Ndinya/Oduor (KEN) d. George Kalanov/Neoklis Neokleous (CYP) 6–3 6–4

PLAYOFF FOR 5TH/6TH POSITIONS

Bosnia/Herzegovina defeated Kenya 3–0
Merid Zahirovic (BIH) d. Barry Ndinya (KEN) 6–1 6–2
Kritian Capalik (BIH) d. Allan Cooper (KEN) 6–2 6–2
Haris Basalic/Igor Stjepic (BIH) d. Barry Ndinya/Norbert Oduor (KEN) 6–2 6–3

PLAYOFF FOR 7TH/8TH POSITIONS

Madagascar defeated Cyprus 3–0
Harivony Andrianafetra (MAD) d. Neoklis Neokleous (CYP) 6–4 6–1
Andriamirija Rajoabelina (MAD) d. George Kalanov (CYP) 7–6(2) 7–5
Jean-Marc Randriamanalina/Germain Rasolondrazana (MAD) d. Marinos
Baghdatis/Demetrios Leondis (CYP) 6–3 4–6 6–2

*Final Positions: 1 Greece, 2 Togo, 3 Estonia, 4 Ghana, 5 Bosnia/Herzegovina, 6 Kenya, 7
Madagascar, 8 Cyprus*

Euro/African Zone B
20–24 May, Skopje, FYR of Macedonia

GROUP A

Turkey defeated San Marino 3–0
Erhan Oral (TUR) d. Cristian Rosti (SMR) 7–6(4) 6–3
Efe Ustundag (TUR) d. Domenico Vicini (SMR) 6–3 4–6 6–3
Mustafa Azkara/Erhal Oral (TUR) d. William Forcellini/Domenico Vicini (SMR) 6–1 6–1
Nigeria defeated Malta 2–1
Jonathan Igbinovia (NGR) d. Mark Schembri (MLT) 6–2 7–6(5)
Sule Ladipo (NGR) d. Christopher Gatt (MLT) 7–5 6–3
Gordon Asiak/Mark Schembri (MLT) d. Ganiyu Adelekan/Yakubu Suleiman (NGR) 6–3 5–7 6–4

Turkey defeated Malta 2–1
Erhan Oral (TUR) d. Mark Schembri (MLT) 7–5 7–6(6)
Christopher Gatt (MLT) d. Efe Ustundag (TUR) 7–6(6) 7–5
Mustafa Azkara/Erhan Oral (TUR) d. Gordon Asciak/Mark Schembri (MLT) 6–4 6–2
Nigeria defeated San Marino 3–0
Jonathan Igbinovia (NGR) d. Cristian Rosti (SMR) 7–6(4) 1–6 6–3
Sule Ladipo (NGR) d. Domenico Vicini (SMR) 5–7 7–6(4) 6–1
Ganiyu Adelekan/Yakubu Suleiman (NGR) d. Cristian Rosti/Domenico Vicini (SMR) 6–3 6–2

Malta defeated San Marino 2–1
Gordon Asciak (MLT) d. Cristian Rosti (SMR) 6–2 1–0 ret.
Domenico Vicini (SMR) d. Christopher Gatt (MLT) 6–3 7–5
Gordon Asciak/Mark Schembri (MLT) d. William Forcellini/Domenico Vicini (SMR) 6–3 6–3
Nigeria defeated Turkey 3–0
Jonathan Igbinovia (NGR) d. Mustafa Azkara (TUR) 7–5 6–7(2) 9–7
Sule Ladipo (NGR) d. Erhan Oral (TUR) 3–6 7–5 6–3
Ganyui Adelekan/Yakubu Suleiman (NGR) d. Haluk Akkoyun/Efe Ustundag (TUR) 6–2 6–3

GROUP B

FYR of Macedonia defeated Tunisia 2–1
Zoran Sevcenko (MKD) d. Selim Baccar (TUN) 6–4 6–1
Oualid Jallali (TUN) d. Ognen Nikolovski (MKD) 6–3 6–4
Lazar Magdincev/Zoran Sevcenk (MKD) d. Selim Baccar/Oualid Jallali (TUN) 6–2 6–3
Moldova defeated Lithuania 2–1
Iuri Gorban (MDA) d. Aistis Slajus (LTU) 6–0 6–3
Rolandos Murashka (LTU) d. Evgueni Plougarev (MDA) 6–2 6–4
Iuri Gorban/Evgueni Plougarev (MDA) d. Rolandos Murashka/Tomas Petrouskas (LTU) 4–6
6–3 9–7

FYR of Macedonia defeated Moldova 2–1
Zoran Sevcenko (MKD) d. Iuri Gorban (MDA) 6–4 6–4
Evgueni Plougarev (MDA) d. Dragan Jovanovski (MDA) 6–4 7–6(5)
Lazar Magdincev/Zoran Sevcenko (MKD) d. Iuri Gorban/Evgueni Plougarev (MDA) 6–2 6–1
Lithuania defeated Tunisia 3–0
Aistis Slajus (LTU) d. Selim Baccar (TUN) 6–4 6–3
Rolandos Murashka (LTU) d. Oualid Jallali (TUN) 6–3 6–0
Rolandos Murashka/Aistis Slajus (LTU) d. Aref Jallali/Issam Jallali (TUN) 6–2 6–1

Lithuania defeated FYR of Macedonia 2–1
Zoran Sevcenko(MKD) d. Aistis Slajus (LTU) 6–2 6–4
Rolandos Murashka (LTU) d. Lazar Magdincev (MKD) 7–6(4) 6–3
Rolandos Murashka/Aistis Slajus (LTU) d. Lazar Magdincev/Zoran Sevcenko (MKD) 3–6 7–5 8–6
Moldova defeated Tunisia 2–1
Iuri Gorban (MDA) d. Issam Jallali (TUN) 6–1 6–0
Oualid Jallali (TUN) d. Evgueni Plougarev (MDA) 7–5 6–4
Victor Ribas/Oleg Sinic (MDA) d. Issam Jallali/Oualid Jallali (TUN) 7–5 6–3

SEMIFINALS

FYR of Macedonia defeated Nigeria 2–1
Zoran Sevcenko (MKD) d. Jonathan Igbinovia (NGR) 6–1 6–4
Sule Ladipo (NGR) d. Lazar Magdincev (MKD) 6–2 6–4
Lazar Magdincev/Zoran Sevcenko (MKD) d. Sule Ladipo/Yakubu Suleiman (NGR) 6–7(4)
7–6(1) 6–4
Turkey defeated Lithuania 2–1
Erhan Oral (TUR) d. Aistis Slajus (LTU) 6–0 6–0
Rolandos Murashka (LTU) d. Efe Ustundag (TUR) 6–3 6–1
Mustafa Azkara/Erhan Oral (TUR) d. Rolandos Murashka/Aistis Slajus (LTU) 6–3 6–4

FINAL

Turkey defeated FYR of Macedonia 3–0
Erhan Oral (TUR) d. Dragan Jovanovski (MKD) 6–0 6–1
Efe Ustundag (TUR) d. Ognen Nikolovski (MKD) 6–1 6–2
Mustafa Azkara/Erhan Oral (TUR) d. Lazar Magdincev/Zoran Sevcenko (MKD) 7–6(4) 7–6(4)

PLAYOFF FOR 3RD/4TH POSITIONS

Lithuania defeated Nigeria 2–1
Tomas Petrouskas (LTU) d. Yakubu Suleiman (NGR) 3–1 ret.
Jonathan Igbinovia (NGR) d. Aistis Slajus (LTU) 6–7(5) 6–1 6–1
Rolandos Murashka/Tomas Petrouskas (LTU) d. Ganiyu Adelekan/Jonathan Igbinovia (NGR)
7–6(4) 6–4

PLAYOFF FOR 5TH–8TH POSITIONS

Tunisia defeated Malta 2–1
Gordon Asciak (MLT) d. Issam Jallali (TUN) 6–2 6–4
Oualid Jallali (TUN) d. Christopher Gatt (MLT) 7–6(4) 6–4
Issam Jallali/Oualid Jallali (TUN) d. Gordon Asciak/Mark Schembri (MLT) 6–4 7–6(4)
Moldova defeated San Marino 2–1
Iuri Gorban (MDA) d. William Forcellini (SMR) 6–2 6–0
Domenico Vicini (SMR) d. Evgueni Plougarev (MDA) 6–3 6–7(5) 7–5
Victor Ribas/Oleg Sinic (MDA) d. Cristian Rosti/Domenico Vicini (SMR) 6–3 6–4

PLAYOFF FOR 5TH/6TH POSITIONS

Tunisia defeated Moldova 2–1
Iuri Gorban (MDA) d. Issam Jallali (TUN) 6–2 7–5
Oualid Jallali (TUN) d. Evgueni Plougarev (MDA) 6–3 1–6 6–2
Issam Jallali/Oualid Jallali (TUN) d. Victor Ribas/Oleg Sinic (MDA) 6–4 7–6(7).

PLAYOFF FOR 7TH/8TH POSITIONS

San Marino defeated Malta 2–1
Mark Schembri (MLT) d. William Forcellini (SMR) 6–3 6–1
Domenico Vicini (SMR) d. Marco Cappello (MLT) 6–3 7–5
Cristian Rosti/Domenico Vicini (SMR) d. Gordon Asciak/Mark Schembri (MLT) 7–6(5) 6–2

*Final Positions: 1 Turkey, 2 FYR of Macedonia, 3 Lithuania, 4 Nigeria, 5 Tunisia, 6 Moldova, 7
San Marino, 8 Malta*

American Zone
29 April–3 May, Santa Cruz, Bolivia

GROUP A

Bolivia defeated Antigua/Barbuda 2–1
Rodrigo Villaroel (BOL) d. Jerry Williams (ANT) 7–6(6) 6–2
Phillip Williamson (ANT) d. Carlos Navarro (BOL) 6–4 6–3
Carlos Navarro/Javier Taborga (BOL) d. Fitroy Anthony/Phillip Williamson (ANT) 5–7 6–4 6–4
Costa Rica defeated Puerto Rico 3–0
Kenneth Thome (CRC) d. Ernie Fernandez (PUR) 7–5 6–4
Federico Camacho (CRC) d. Luis Haddock (PUR) 6–2 6–4
Federico Camacho/Kenneth Thome (CRC) d. Ernie Fernandez/Edgardo Rivera (PUR) 6–3 6–4

Puerto Rico defeated Antigua/Barbuda 2–1
Ernie Fernandez (PUR) d. Fitzroy Anthony (ANT) 6–2 6–1
Phillip Williamson (ANT) d. Luis Haddock (PUR) 6–4 6–1
Ernie Fernandez/Edgardo Rivera (PUR) d. Jerry Williams/Phillip Williamson (ANT) 4–6 7–6(4) 6–3
Costa Rica defeated Bolivia 2–1
Rafael Brenes (CRC) d. Rodrigo Villaroel (BOL) 6–2 6–4
Jose Antelo (BOL) d. Federico Camacho (CRC) 7–6(2) 6–3
Rafael Brenes/Kenneth Thome (CRC) d. Carlos Navarro/Javier Taborga (BOL) 2–6 6–1 6–4

Bolivia defeated Puerto Rico 3–0
Jose Antelo (BOL) d. Gilberto Rivera (PUR) 6–2 7–6(5)
Carlos Navarro (BOL) d. Luis Haddock (PUR) 6–0 6–1
Javier Taborga/Rodrigo Villaroel (BOL) d. Luis Haddock/Edgardo Rivera (PUR) 6–3 6–2
Costa Rica defeated Antigua/Barbuda 2–1
Federico Camacho (CRC) d. Jerry Williams (ANT) 6–0 6–0
Phillip Williamson (ANT) d. Fabrizio Golfin (CRC) 6–2 6–2
Rafael Brenes/Kenneth Thome (CRC) d. Fitzroy Anthony/Desney Williams (ANT) 6–4 6–2

GROUP B

El Salvador defeated Bermuda 2–1
Miguel Merz (ESA) d. James Collieson (BER) 7–5 6–3
Donald Evans (BER) d. Jose Baires (ESA) 6–4 5–7 6–3
Yari Bernardo/Miguel Merz (ESA) d. Ricky Mallory/Michael Way (BER) 6–2 6–4
Dominican Republic defeated Panama 2–1
Chad Valdez (PAN) d. Sixto Camacho (DOM) 6–3 7–5
Rodrigo Vallejo (DOM) d. Carlos Silva (PAN) 6–4 6–4
Sixto Camacho/Rodrigo Vallejo (DOM) d. Jan Gelabert/Chad Valdez (PAN) 4–6 6–3 6–2

El Salvador defeated Panama 3–0
Yari Bernardo (ESA) d. Chad Valdez (PAN) 6–4 6–3
Miguel Merz (ESA) d. Carlos Silva (PAN) 7–5 6–2
Jose Baires/Yari Bernardo (ESA) d. Jean Gelabert/Abad Goon (PAN) 6–4 6–7(2) 8–6
Dominican Republic defeated Bermuda 2–1
Sixto Camacho (DOM) d. Michael Way (BER) 4–6 6–1 6–3
Rodrigo Vallejo (DOM) d. James Collieson (BER) 6–1 6–0
James Collieson/Donald Evans (BER) d. Victor Estrella/Johnson Garcia (DOM) 4–6 6–3 7–5

Dominican Republic defeated El Salvador 2–1
Yari Bernardo (ESA) d. Johnson Garcia (DOM) 6–7(4) 6–3 8–6
Rodrigo Vallejo (DOM) d. Manuel Tejada (ESA) 6–2 6–4
Sixto Camacho/Rodrigo Vallejo (DOM) d. Miguel Merz/Manuel Tejada (ESA) 0–30 ret.
Bermuda defeated Panama 2–1
Carlos Silva (PAN) d. James Collieson (BER) 4–6 6–0 6–3
Donald Evans (BER) d. Abad Goon (PAN) 6–3 7–6(2)
Ricky Mallory/Michael Way (BER) d. Jean Gelabert/Abad Goon (PAN) 7–5 7–5

SEMIFINALS

Dominican Republic defeated Bolivia 2–0
Johnson Garcia (DOM) d. Jose Antelo (BOL) 2–6 6–4 6–4
Rodrigo Vallejo (DOM) d. Carlos Navarro (BOL) 6–0 7–6(5)
Costa Rica defeated El Salvador 2–1
Miguel Merz (ESA) d. Rafael Brenes (CRC) 6–4 6–2
Kenneth Thome (CRC) d. Jose Baires (ESA) 6–3 6–3
Rafael Brenes/Kenneth Thome (CRC) d. Yari Bernardo/Miguel Merz (ESA) 7–6(4) 6–2

FINAL

Dominican Republic defeated Costa Rica 2–1
Johnson Garcia (DOM) d. Rafael Brenes (CRC) 7–6(3) 6–2
Rodrigo Vallejo (DOM) d. Federico Camacho (CRC) 6–2 7–5
Rafael Brenes/Kenneth Thome (CRC) d. Sixto Camacho/Victor Estrella (DOM) 6–4 7–6(3)

PLAYOFF FOR 3RD/4TH POSITIONS

El Salvador defeated Bolivia 3–0
Yari Bernardo (ESA) d. Javier Taborga (BOL) 7–5 6–4
Jose Baires (ESA) d. Carlos Navarro (BOL) 0–6 6–3 14–12
Jose Baires/Miguel Merz (ESA) d. Javier Taborga/Rodrigo Villaroel (BOL) 5–7 6–2 6–4

PLAYOFF FOR 5TH–8TH POSITIONS

Panama defeated Puerto Rico 2–0
Chad Valdez (PAN) d. Ernie Fernandez (PUR) 6–7(6) 6–2 6–4
Carlos Silva (PAN) d. Edgardo Rivera (PUR) 6–0 1–6 10–8
Antigua/Barbuda defeated Bermuda 2–1
Michael Way (BER) d. Jerry Williams (ANT) 6–2 4–6 6–3
Phillip Williamson (ANT) d. James Collieson (BER) 6–0 6–3
Jerry Williams/Phillip Williamson (ANT) d. Donald Evans/Ricky Mallory (BER) 6–3 6–4

PLAYOFF FOR 5TH/6TH POSITIONS

Panama defeated Antigua/Barbuda 2–1
Chad Valdez (PAN) d. Jerry Williams (ANT) 6–3 6–0
Phillip Williamson (ANT) d. Carlos Silva (PAN) 6–3 6–3
Abad Goon/Chad Valdez (PAN) d. Desney Williams/Phillip Williamson (ANT) 6–4 6–4

PLAYOFF FOR 7TH/8TH POSITIONS

Puerto Rico defeated Bermuda 2–1
Gilberto Rivera (PUR) d. James Collieson (BER) 7–5 2–6 10–8
Luis Haddock (PUR) d. Donald Evans (BER) 6–3 7–6(1)
Donald Evans/ Ricky Mallory (BER) d. Luis Haddock/Edgardo Rivera (PUR) 6–3 6–7(6) 6–1

Final Positions: 1 Dominican Republic, 2 Costa Rica, 3 El Salvador, 4 Bolivia, 5 Panama, 6 Antigua/Barbuda, 7 Puerto Rico, 8 Bermuda

Asia/Oceania Zone
15–19 April, Kuala Lumpur, Malaysia

GROUP A

Syria defeated Singapore 2–1
Rabi Bou-Hassoun (SYR) d. Yang-Tat Sherman Lim (SIN) 6–3 6–2
Samir Saad El Din (SYR) d. Ju-Min Adrian Lam (SIN) 6–1 6–2
Jensen Hiu/Leng-Kar Yiu (SIN) d. Lais Salim/Mohamed Jehad Sheet (SYR) 6–2 6–3
Kazakhstan defeated Sri Lanka 3–0
Pavel Baranov (KAZ) d. Rohan De Silva (SRI) 6–4 6–4
Alexei Kedriouk (KAZ) d. Jayendra Wijeyesekera (SRI) 6–3 6–2
Pavel Baranov/Igor Chaldounov (KAZ) d. Rajeev Rajapakse/Samitha Mahinju Ranaweera (SRI) 6–4 6–4

Sri Lanka defeated Syria 2–1
Rabi Bou-Hassoun (SYR) d. Rohan De Silva (SRI) 6–3 6–4
Jayendra Wijeyesekera (SRI) d. Samir Saad El Din (SYR) 4–6 6–1 6–0
Rohan De Silva/Jayendra Wijeyesekera (SRI) d. Rabi Bou-Hassoun/Samir Saad El Din (SYR) 5–7 6–2 6–1
Kazakhstan defeated Singapore 3–0
Pavel Baranov (KAZ) d. Jensen Hiu (SIN) 6–0 5–7 6–4
Alexei Kedriouk (KAZ) d. Yang-Tat Sherman Lim (SIN) 6–3 6–3
Pavel Baranov/Alexei Kedriouk (KAZ) d. Ju-Min Adrian Lam/Yang-Tat Sherman Lim (SIN) 6–2 6–4

Kazakhstan defeated Syria 3–0
Pavel Baranov (KAZ) d. Rabi Bou-Hassoun (SYR) 7–6(4) 6–2 6–3
Alexei Kedriouk (KAZ) d. Samir Saad El Din (SYR) 6–0 6–0
Alexei Kedriouk/Igor Chaldounov (KAZ) d. Lais Salim/Mohamed Jehad Sheet (SYR) 6–2 6–0
Sri Lanka defeated Singapore 3–0
Rohan De Silva (SRI) d. Yang-Tat Sherman Lim (SIN) 6–1 3–6 6–2
Jayendra Wijeyesekera (SRI) d. Leng-Kar Yiu (SIN) 6–0 6–1
Rajeev Rajapakse/Samitha Mahinju Ranaweera (SRI) d. Jensen Hiu/Len-Kar Yiu (SIN) 6–2 7–5

GROUP B

Malaysia defeated Kuwait 2–1
Mohammad Al-Ghareeb (KUW) d. Ramayah Ramachandran (MAS) 4–5 ret.
Selvam Veerasingam (MAS) d. Adel Al-Shatti (KUW) 7–5 7–6(1)
Vasuthevan Ortchuan/Selvam Veerasingam (MAS) d. Mohammad Al-Ghareeb/Adel Al-Shatti (KUW) 6–1 6–3
Saudi Arabia defeated Tajikistan 2–1
Bader-Mohamed Al-Megayel (KSA) d. Sergei Makashin (TJK) 6–3 6–2
Mansour Takhjaev (TJK) d. Othman Saleh Al-Anazi (KSA) 6–2 6–3
Othman Al-Anazi/Bader-Mohamed Al-Megayel (KSA) d. Mansour Takhjaev/Bakhrullo Radjabalien (TJK) 6–4 6–0

Malaysia defeated Saudi Arabia 2–1
Bader-Mohamed Al-Megayel (KSA) d. Vasuthevan Ortchuan (MAS) 4–6 6–3 6–2
Selvam Veerasingam (MAS) d. Othman Saleh Al-Anazi (KSA) 6–2 6–4
Vasuthevan Ortchuan/Selvam Veerasingam (MAS) d. Othman Saleh Al-Anazi/Bader-Mohamed Al-Megayel (KSA) 6–4 6–3
Tajikistan defeated Kuwait 2–1
Mohammad Al-Ghareeb (KUW) d. Sergei Makashin (TJK) 6–3 6–3
Mansour Takhjaev (TJK) d. Adel Al-Shatti (KUW) 6–2 6–3
Sergei Makashin/Mansour Takhjaev (TJK) d. Mohammad Al-Ghareeb/Adel Al-Shatti (KUW) 6–4 6–4

Tajikistan defeated Malaysia 2–1
Sergei Makashin (TJK) d. Abdul Aziz Shazali (MAS) 6–1 6–1
Mansour Takhjaev (TJK) d. Selvam Veerasingam (MAS) 7–6(6) 7–6(13)
Vasuthevan Ortchuan/Selvam Veerasingam (MAS) d. Sergei Makashin/Mansour Takhjaev (TJK) 7–6(2) 6–1
Saudi Arabia defeated Kuwait 2–1
Bader-Mohamed Al-Megayel (KSA) d. Hussain Al-Ghareeb (KUW) 6–3 4–6 6–2
Mohammad Al-Ghareeb (KUW) d. Othman Saleh Al-Anazi (KSA) 6–3 6–4
Bader-Mohamed Al-Megayel /Fareh Al-Somali (KSA) d. Mohammad Al-Ghareeb/Adel Al-Shatti (KUW) 7–6(4) 6–2

SEMIFINALS

Kazakhstan defeated Tajikistan 3–0
Pavel Baranov (KAZ) d. Sergei Makashin (TJK) 6–2 6–4
Alexei Kedriouk (KAZ) d. Mansoour Takhjaev (TJK) 7–6(2) 6–1
Pavel Baranov/Igor Chaldounov (KAZ) d. Roustam Amonov/Sergei Makashin (TJK) 6–2 6–3
Sri Lanka defeated Malaysia 2–1
Rohan De Silva (SRI) d. Vasuthevan Ortchuan (MAS) 6–2 6–3
Selvam Veerasingam (MAS) d. Jayendra Wijeyesekera (SRI) 7–5 6–1
Rohand De Silva/Jayendra Wijeyesekera (SRI) d. Ramayah Ramachandran/Selvam Veerasingam (MAS) 0–6 7–5 6–3

FINAL

Kazakhstan defeated Sri Lanka 3–0
Pavel Baranov (KAZ) d. Rajeev Rajapakse (SRI) 6–3 6–1
Alexei Kedriouk (KAZ) d. Samitha Mahinju Ranaweera (SRI) 6–1 6–3
Pavel Baranov/Igor Chaldounov (KAZ) d. Rajeev Rajapakse/Samitha Mahinju Ranaweera (SRI) 7–5 6–0

PLAYOFF FOR 3RD/4TH POSITIONS

Tajikistan defeated Malaysia 3–0
Sergei Makashin (TJK) d. Abdul Aziz Shazali (MAS) 6–4 6–1
Mansour Takhjaev (TJK) d. Vasuthevan Ortchuan (MAS) 6–1 6–3
Sergei Makashin/Mansour Takhjaev (TJK) d. Vasuthevan Ortchuan/Abdul Aziz Shazali (MAS) 7–6(4) 6–2

PLAYOFF FOR 5TH–8TH POSITIONS

Syria defeated Kuwait 2–1
Rabi Bou-Hassoun (SYR) d. Mohammad Al-Ghareeb (KUW) 6–4 6–4
Samir Saad El Din (SYR) d. Adel Al-Shatti (KUW) 6–3 6–1
Hussain Al-Ghareeb/Ali Hayat (KUW) d. Lais Salim/Mohamed Jehad Sheet (SYR) 7–6(8) 6–3
Saudi Arabia defeated Singapore 2–1
Bader-Mohamed Al-Megayel (KSA) d. Jensen Hiu (SIN) 6–0 6–2
Yang-Tat Sherman Lim (SIN) d. Othman Saleh Al-Anazi (KSA) 6–3 6–3
Bader-Mohamed Al-Megayel/Fareh Al-Somali (KSA) d. Ju-Min Adrian Lam/Yang-Tat Sherman Lim (SIN) 7–6(3) 6–2

PLAYOFF FOR 5TH/6TH POSITIONS

Syria defeated Saudi Arabia 3–0
Rabi Bou-Hassoun (SYR) d. Fareh Al-Somali (KSA) 6–3 6–2
Sami Saad El Din (SYR) d. Moafa Tawfiq (KSA) 6–2 6–0
Lais Salim/Mohamed Jehad Sheet (SYR) d. Fareh Al-Somali/Moafa Tawfiq (KSA) 6–3 6–3

PLAYOFF FOR 7TH/8TH POSITIONS

Singapore defeated Kuwait 2–1
Jensen Hiu (SIN) d. Ali Hayat (KUW) 6–2 6–2
Hussain Al-Ghareeb (KUW) d. Leng-Kar Yiu (SIN) 2–6 6–3 6–4
Jensen Hiu/Leng-Kar Yiu (SIN) d. Hussain Al-Ghareeb/Ali Hayat (KUW) 6–4 6–1

Final Positions: 1 Kazakhstan, 2 Sri Lanka, 3 Tajikistan, 4 Malaysia, 5 Syria, 6 Saudi Arabia, 7 Singapore, 8 Kuwait

Group IV

Euro/African Zone A
28 January–1 February, Kampala, Uganda

GROUP A

Armenia defeated Uganda 2–1
Tsolak Gevorgyan (ARM) d. Charles Yokwe (UGA) 6–0 6–0
Sargius Sargsian (ARM) d. John Oduke (UGA) 6–2 6–4
John Oduke/Renato Sebbi (UGA) d. Davit Babayan/Haik Hakobyan (ARM) 6–1 6–3
Benin defeated Djibouti 3–0
Sourou Gandonou (BEN) d. Abdou-Rahman Omar (DJI) 6–1 6–0
Christophe Pognon (BEN) d. Omar Awad Mohammed (DJI) 6–0 6–0
Jean-Marie Da Silva/Alphonse Gandonou (BEN) d. Ali Aden/Kadar Mohamed (DJI) 6–0 6–1

Armenia defeated Djibouti 2–0
Tsolak Gevorgyan (ARM) d. Ali Aden (DJI) 6–0 6–0
Sargius Sargsian (ARM) d. Abdou-Rahman Omar (DJI) 6–0 6–0
Doubles not played due to bad weather

Benin defeated Uganda 2–0
Sourou Gandonou (BEN) d. Renato Sebbi (UGA) 6–1 6–2
Christophe Pognon (BEN) d. John Oduke (UGA) 4–6 6–2 6–3
Doubles not played due to bad weather

Armenia defeated Benin 2–1
Tsolak Gevorgyan (ARM) d. Sourou Gandonou (BEN) 5–7 7–6(4) 6–2
Sargius Sargsian (ARM) d. Christophe Pognon (BEN) 6–0 6–2
Jean-Marie Da Silva/Alphonse Gandonou (BEN) d. Davit Babayan/Haik Hakobyan (ARM) 6–3 6–4
Uganda defeated Djibouti 3–0
Robert Buyinza (UGA) d. Kadar Mohamed (DJI) 6–0 6–2
John Oduke (UGA) d. Ali Aden (DJI) 6–0 6–0
Renato Sebbi/Charles Yokwe (UGA) d. Omar-Awad Mohammed/Abdou-Rahman Omar (DJI) 6–0 6–4

GROUP B

Botswana defeated Azerbaijan 3–0
Michael Judd (BOT) d. Dmitri Zaraubin (AZE) 6–2 6–3
Petrus Molefhe (BOT) d. Igor Borisov (AZE) 6–2 6–4
Michael Judd/Thato Kgosimore (BOT) d. Raouf Eyvazov/Eldar Kafarov (AZE) 6–3 6–2
Cameroon defeated Sudan 3–0
Michel Ekwe (CMR) d. Mandour Abdalla (SUD) 7–6(7) 6–7(6) 12–10
Abel Lobe Tabi (CMR) d. Nour El Din Gaafar (SUD) 7–5 6–3
Maurice Fomete/Simplice Meng (CMR) d. Mogeeb Abdalla/Asim-Omer El Agraa (SUD) 6–4 6–2

Botswana defeated Sudan 2–0
Thato Kgosimore (BOT) d. Mandour Abdalla (SUD) 4–6 7–6(5) 6–2
Petrus Molefhe (BOT) d. Nour El Din Gaafar (SUD) 6–0 6–2
Doubles not played due to bad weather
Cameroun defeated Azerbaijan 2–0
Michel Ekwe (CMR) d. Dmitri Zaraubin (AZE) 7–5 6–4
Abel Lobe Tabi (CMR) d. Igor Borisov (AZE) 6–4 3–6 6–3
Doubles not played due to bad weather

Cameroun defeated Botswana 2–1
Michel Ekwe (CMR) d. Michael Judd (BOT) 7–5 6–4
Petrus Molefhe (BOT) d. Abel Lobe Tabi (CMR) 7–6(3) 3–6 6–2
Michel Ekwe/Maurice Fomete (CMR) d. Michael Judd/Thato Kgosimore (BOT) 6–4 6–4
Azerbaijan defeated Sudan 2–1
Raouf Eyvazov (AZE) d. Asim-Omer Abdul-Rahma El Agraa (SUD) 6–2 5–7 6–4
Mandour Abdalla (SUD) d. Dmitri Zaraubin (AZE) 6–3 7–6(2)
Igor Borisov/Raouf Eyvazov (ARM) d. Mandour Abdalla/Mogeeb Abdalla (SUD) 7–6(6) 6–2

SEMIFINALS

Armenia defeated Botswana 2–1
Tsolak Gevorgyan (ARM) d. Michael Judd (BOT) 6–2 6–2
Sargius Sargsian (ARM) d. Petrus Molefhe (BOT) 6–2 6–3
Michael Judd/Thato Kgosimore (BOT) d. Davit Babayan/Haik Hakobyan (ARM) 4–6 7–5 8–6
Benin defeated Cameroun 2–1
Sourou Gandonou (BEN) d. Simplice Meng (CMR) 6–3 1–0 ret.
Christophe Pognon (BEN) d. Michel Ekwe (CMR) 7–6(7) 6–2
Maurice Fomete/Abel Lobi Tabi (CMR) d. Alphonse Gandonou/Sourou Gandonou (BEN) 1–6 6–2 6–2

FINAL

Armenia defeated Benin 3–0
w/o

PLAYOFF FOR 3RD/4TH POSITIONS

Botswana defeated Cameroun 3–0
Thato Kgosimore (BOT) d. Michel Ekwe (CMR) 6–3 6–3
Petrus Molefhe (BOT) d. Maurice Fomete (CMR) 6–1 6–4
Michael Judd/Thato Kgosimore (BOT) d. Maurice Fomete/Abel Lobe Tabi (CMR) 6–3 6–2

PLAYOFF FOR 5TH–8TH POSITIONS

Uganda defeated Sudan 3–0
Robert Buyinza (UGA) d. Asim-Omer El Agraa (SUD) 6–1 6–4
John Oduke (UGA) d. Nour El Din Gaafar (SUD) 6–0 6–0
Robert Buyinza/Renato Sebbi (UGA) d. Mogeeb Abdalla/Nour El Din Gaafar (SUD) 7–6(6) 5–7 8–6
Azerbaijan defeated Djibouti 3–0
Eldar Kafarov (AZE) d. Kadar Mohamed (DJI) 6–4 6–1
Raouf Eyvazov (AZE) d. Ali Aden (DJI) 6–1 6–0
Igor Borisov/Raouf Eyvazov (AZE) d. Kadar Mohamed/Abdou-Rahman Omar (DJI) 6–1 6–1

PLAYOFF FOR 5TH/6TH POSITIONS

Uganda defeated Azerbaijan 2–1
Dmitri Zaraubin (AZE) d. Robert Buyinza (UGA) 6–3 6–2
John Oduke (UGA) d. Igor Borisov (AZE) 7–5 5–7 6–4
John Oduke/Renato Sebbi (UGA) d. Raouf Eyvazov/Dmitri Zaraubin (AZE) 6–3 6–4

PLAYOFF FOR 7TH/8TH POSITIONS

Sudan defeated Djibouti 3–0
Mandour Abdalla (SUD) d. Abdou-Rahman Omar (DJI) 6–0 6–0
Nour El Din Gaafar (SUD) d. Omar-Awad Mohammed (DJI) 6–1 6–0
Mogeeb Abdalla/Omar-Awad Mohammed (SUD) d. Ali Aden/Kadar Mohamed (DJI) 6–0 6–0

Final Positions: 1 Armenia, 2 Benin, 3 Botswana, 4 Cameroun, 5 Uganda, 6 Azerbaijan, 7 Sudan, 8 Djibouti

Euro/African Zone B
4–10 May, Nobla, Zambia

Zambia defeated Ethiopia 3–0
Sidney Bwalya (ZAM) d. Yohannes Setegne (ETH) 6–3 6–3
Lighton Ndefway (ZAM) d. Samuel Gabriel (ETH) 3–6 6–1 6–2
Kachinga Sinkala/Dermot Sweeney (ZAM) d. Asfawe Michaile/Yohannes Setegne (ETH) 6–2 6–2

Algeria defeated Liechtenstein 3–0
Nourredine Mahmoudi (ALG) d. Jurgen Tomordy (LIE) 7–6(3) 4–6 6–3
Abdelhak Hameurlaine (ALG) d. Stephan Ritter (LIE) 3–6 6–1 86 Sid Ali Akkal/Nourredine Mahmoudi (ALG) d. Frank Heeb/Rainer Kovac (LIE) 6–3 2–6 6–1

Ethiopia defeated Liechtenstein 2–1
Yohannes Setegne (ETH) d. Jurgen Tomordy (LIE) 6–3 6–3
Stephan Ritter (LIE) d. Samuel Gabriel (ETH) 6–4 6–2
Asfawe Michaile/Yohannes Setegne (ETH) d. Rainer Kovac/Stephan Ritter (LIE) 6–3 1–6 6–4

Zambia defeated Iceland 3–0
Dermot Sweeney (ZAM) d. Einar-Axel Sigurgeirsson (ISL) 4–6 6–3 6–4
Lighton Ndefway (ZAM) d. Raj Bonifacius (ISL) 6–4 6–2
Kachinga Sinkala/Dermot SWEeney (ZAM) d. Gunnar Einarsson/David Halldorsson (ISL) 4–6 6–3 6–2

Algeria defeated Ethiopia 2–1
Mohamed Mahmoudi (ALG) d. Yohannes Setegne (ETH) 3–6 6–1 6–4
Abdelhak Hameurlaine (ALG) d. Samuel Gabriel (ETH) 6–2 6–1
Asfawe Michaile/Yohannes Setegne (ETH) d. Sid Ali Akkal/Nourredine Mahmoudi (ALG) 5–7 6–4 6–2

Iceland defeated Liechtenstein 2–1
Einar-Axel Sigurgeirsson (ISL) d. Jurgen Tomordy (LIE) 6–0 6–1
Stephan Ritter (LIE) d. Raj Bonifacius (ISL) 6–2 4–6 6–1
Gunnar Einarsson/David Halldorsson (ISL) d. Rainer Kovac/Stephan Ritter (LIE) 7–6(4) 4–6 8–6

Zambia defeated Liechtenstein 3–0
Sidney Bwalya (ZAM) d. Frank Heeb (LIE) 6–1 6–0
Dermot SWEeney (ZAM) d. Stephan Ritter (LIE) 6–4 6–3
Sidney Bwalya/Kachinga Sinkala (ZAM) d. Frank Heeb/Rainer Kovac (LIE) 6–2 7–6(0)

Algeria defeated Iceland 3–0
Nourredine Mahmoudi (ALG) d. Gunnar Einarsson (ISL) 7–5 4–6 6–1
Abdelhak Hameurlaine (ALG) d. Einar-Axel Sigurgeirsson (LIE) 6–7(6) 6–0 6–4
Abdelhak Hameurlaine/Mohamed Mahmoudi (ALG) d. Raj Bonifacius/David Halldorsson (ISL) 6–2 6–4

Zambia defeated Algeria 2–1
Sidney Bwalya (ZAM) d. Mohamed Mahmoudi (ALG) 6–3 6–2
Abdelhak Hameurlaine (ALG) d. Kachinga Sinkala (ZAM) 1–6 6–3 6–4
Sidney Bwalya/Lighton Ndefway (ZAM) d. Abdelhak Hameurlaine/Mourredine Mahmoudi (ALG) 6–4 6–3

Ethiopia defeated Iceland 2–1
Yohannes Setegne (ETH) d. Gunnar Einarsson (ISL) 6–3 7–6(1)
Einar-Axel Sigurgeirsson (ISL) d. Samuel Gabriel (ETH) 6–1 6–1
Asfawe Michaile/Yohannes Setegne (ETH) d. Raj Bonifacius/Einar-Axel Sigurgeirsson (ISL) 2–6 6–3 6–4

Final Positions: 1 Zambia, 2 Algeria, 3 Ethiopia, 4 Iceland, 5 Liechtenstein

American Zone
23–29 March, St Lucia

Honduras defeated Barbados 2–1
Calton Alvarez (HON) d. James Betts (BAR) 3–6 6–2 6–3
Carlos Caceres (HON) d. Duane Williams (BAR) 6–2 6–2
Bernard Frost/Kodi Lewis (BAR) d. Carlos Caceres/Franklin Garcia (HON) 3–6 6–4 7–5

US Virgin Islands defeated Trinidad & Tobago 3–0
Wilbur Callender Jr (ISV) d. Ronald Greaves (TRI) 7–6(3) 6–2
Eugene Highfield (ISV) d. Floyd Williams (TRI) 6–1 6–2
Eugene Highfield/Morris Brown (ISV) d. Stephan George/Brian Khan (TRI) 6–3 6–2

Netherlands Antilles defeated OECS 3–0
Jean Julien Rojer (AHO) d. Nigel Liverpool (ECA) 6–3 7–6(5)
Elmar Gerth (AHO) d. Kirsten Cable (ECA) 6–1 6–0
Elmar Gerth/Kevin Jonckheer (AHO) d. Nigel Liverpool/Peter Nanton (ECA) 6–2 6–1

St Lucia defeated OECS 2–1
Vernon Lewis (LCA) d. Nigel Liverpool (ECA) 6–1 6–2
Henri Sinson (LCA) d. Kirsten Cable (ECA) 6–1 6–3
Haydon Ashton/Kirsten Cable (ECA) d. Kane Easter/Glynne James (LCA) 3–6 7–5 6–4

Netherlands Antilles defeated US Virgin Islands 3–0
Jean Julien Rojer (AHO) d. Wilbur Callender Jr (ISV) 6–3 7–5
Elmar Gerth (AHO) d. Eugene Highfield (ISV) 6–4 6–2
Elmar Gerth/Kevin Jonckheer (AHO) d. Morris Brown/George Lewis (ISV) 6–0 6–3

Honduras defeated Trinidad & Tobago 2–1
Carlton Alvarez (HON) d. Brian Khan (TRI) 6–4 6–0
Carlos Caceres (HON) d. Stephen George (TRI) 6–0 6–3
Brian Khan/Floyd Williams (TRI) d. Carlos Caceres/Franklin Garcia (HON) 6–3 6–4

St Lucia defeated US Virgin Islands 3–0
Kane Easter (LCA) d. Morris Brown (ISV) 6–4 7–5
Vernon Lewis (LCA) d. Eugene Highfield (ISV) 6–1 6–4
Glynne James/Henri Sinson (LCA) d. Wilbur Callender Jr/George Lewis (ISV) 6–3 6–2

Netherlands Antilles defeated Barbados 3–0
Jean Julien Rojer (AHO) d. James Betts (BAR) 6–0 7–5
Elmar Gerth (AHO) d. Duane Williams (BAR) 6–0 6–1
Elmar Gerth/Kevin Jonckheer (AHO) d. Bernard Frost/Kodi Lewis (BAR) 6–1 6–3

Trinidad & Tobago defeated OECS 3–0
Brian Khan (TRI) d. Nigel Liverpool (ECA) 6–3 6–2
Ronald Greaves (TRI) d. Hayden Ashton (ECA) 6–1 6–0
Brian Khan/Floyd Williams (TRI) d. Nigel Liverpool/Peter Nanton (ECA) 6–4 7–5

Trinidad & Tobago defeated St Lucia 2–1
Ronald Greaves (TRI) d. Vernon Lewis (LCA) 7–5 6–0
Henri Sinson (LCA) d. Floyd Williams (TRI) 6–4 7–5
Ronald Greaves/Brian Khan (TRI) d. Glynne James/Henri Sinson (LCA) 6–2 6–2

Honduras defeated US Virgin Islands 2–1
Calton Alvarez (HON) d. Wilbur Callender Jr (ISV) 6–3 1–6 6–2
Carlos Caceres (HON) d. Eugene Highfield (ISV) 6–4 7–6(3)
Wilbur Callender Jr/George Lewis (ISV) d. Franklin Garcia/Humberto Rodriguez (HON) 7–6(2) 7–5

Barbados defeated OECS 2–1
Kodi Lewis (BAR) d. Nigel Liverpool (ECA) 4–6 6–3 6–2
Bernard Frost (BAR) d. Kirsten Cable (ECA) 6–3 6–4
Haydon Ashton/Kirsten Cable (ECA) d. James Betts/Duane Williams (BAR) 3–6 6–3 6–4

Honduras defeated St Lucia 2–1
Calton Alvarez (HON) d. Kane Easter (LCA) 6–4 7–6(4)
Carlos Caceres (HON) d. Vernon Lewis (LCA) 6–1 6–4
Kane Easter/Henri Sinson (LCA) d. Calton Alvarez/Franklin Garcia (HON) 6–1 6–4

Barbados defeated US Virgin Islands 2–1
James Betts (BAR) d. Wilbur Callender Jr (ISV) 7–6(4) 7–5
Eugene Highfield (ISV) d. Duane Williams (BAR) 6–0 6–4
James Betts/Bernard Frost (BAR) d. Eugene Highfield/George Lewis (ISV) 6–3 6–4

Netherlands Antilles defeated Trinidad & Tobago 3–0
Jean Julien Rojer (AHO) d. Brian Khan (TRI) 6–2 6–2
Elmar Gerth (AHO) d. Ronald Greaves (TRI) 6–4 6–4
Elmar Gerth/Kevin Jonckheer (AHO) d. Ronald Greaves/Brian Khan (TRI) 6–0 6–2

St Lucia defeated Barbados 2–1
Kane Easter (LCA) d. James Betts (BAR) 6–3 6–3
Henri Sinson (LCA) d. Bernard Frost (BAR) 6–3 6–3
Bernard Frost/Kodi Lewis (BAR) d. Glynne James/Vernon Lewis (LCA) 3–6 7–6(5) 6–4

Netherlands Antilles defeated Honduras 2–1
Calton Alvarez (HON) d. Jean Julien Rojer (AHO) 7–6(2) 6–1
Elmar Gerth (AHO) d. Carlos Caceres (HON) 6–3 6–2
Elmar Gerth/Kevin Jonckheer (AHO) d. Calton Alvarez/Carlos Caceres (HON) 6–1 6–7(5) 6–1

US Virgin Islands defeated OECS 2–1
Wilbur Callender Jr (ISV) d. Kirsten Cable (ECA) 6–4 6–3
Eugene Highfield (ISV) d. Hayden Ashton (ECA) 6–1 6–4
Hayden Ashton/Kirsten Cable (ECA) d. Wilbur Callender Jr/Eugene Highfield (ISV) 6–4 3–6 10–8

Netherlands Antilles defeated St Lucia 2–1
Vernon Lewis (LCA) d. Jean Julien Rojer (AHO) 3–6 6–1 6–2
Elmar Gerth (AHO) d. Henri Sinson (LCA) 6–2 6–3
Raul Behr/Elmar Gerth (AHO) d. Vernon Lewis/Henri Sinson (LCA) 6–3 7–5

Trinidad & Tobago defeated Barbados 2–1
Brian Khan (TRI) d. Kodi Lewis (BAR) 6–2 6–0
Ronald Greaves (TRI) d. Bernard Frost (BAR) 6–2 4–6 7–5
James Betts/Duane Williams (BAR) d. Stephen George/Floyd Williams (TRI) 6–3 6–7(4) 6–4

Honduras defeated OECS 2–1
Calton Alvarez (HON) d. Kirsten Cable (ECA) 6–0 6–3
Carlos Caceres (HON) d. Haydon Ashton (ECA) 6–1 2–0 ret.
Kirsten Cable/Nigel Liverpool (ECA) d. Calton Alvarez/Franklin Garcia (HON) 4–6 6–3 6–3

Netherlands Antilles and Honduras promoted to American Group III in 1999

Asia/Oceania Zone
9–15 February, Dhaka, Bangladesh

Bangladesh defeated Oman 2–1
Mudrik-Nadhim Al-Rawahi (OMA) d. Dilip Passia (BAN) 7–5 3–6 6–2
Shibu Lal (BAN) d. Khalid Al-Nabhani (OMA) 6–1 6–0
Shibu Lal/Moin-ud-din Walliullah (BAN) d. Khalid Al-Nabhani/Mudrik-Nadhim Al-Rawahi (OMA) 6–3 6–2

Iraq defeated Brunei 3–0
Mohamad Ibrahim (IRQ) d. Aki Ismasufian Bin Pj Haji Ibrahim (BRU) 6–3 6–1
Saddam Hussain Kadhim (IRQ) d. Tony Shim (BRU) 6–0 6–1
Saddam Hussain Kadhim/Hussein Ahmed Rashid (IRQ) d. Aki Ismasufian Bing Pg Haji Ibrahim/Latif Isa (BRU) 6–4 6–2

Bahrain defeated UAE 3–0
Essam-Jaafar Ali Abdul-Aal (BRN) d. Mahmoud Nader Al-Baloushi (UAE) 6–1 6–0
Abdul-Latif Ahmed (BRN) d. Othman Al-Ulama (UAE) 6–3 6–1
Mohamed Jasim Sanad Ahmed/Abdul-Latif Ahmed (BRN) d. Mahmoud Nader Al-Baloushi/Mohammed Jamal Buschager (UAE) 6–1 6–0

Bahrain defeated Oman 3–0
Essam-Jaafar Ali Abdul- Aal (BRN) d. Mazin Al-Shaibani (OMA) 6–0 6–0
Abdul-Latif Ahmed (BRN) d. Mudrik-Nadhim Al-Rawahi (OMA) 6–1 3–6 6–4
Essam-Jaafar Ali Abdul-Aal/Mohamed Jasim Sanad Ahmed (BRN) d. Khalid Al-Nabhani/Barkat-Salim Al-Sharji (OMA) 6–3 6–2

Bangladesh defeated UAE 3–0
Dilip Passia (BAN) d. Mahmoud Nader Al-Baloushi (UAE) 6–2 6–3
Shibu Lal (BAN) d. Othman Al-Ulama (UAE) 6–0 6–1
Muammer Husain Khan/Moin-ud-din Walliullah (BAN) d. Mahmoud Nader Al-Baloushi/Mohammed-Saeed Al-Marri (UAE) 6–3 6–2

Jordan defeated Brunei 3–0
Fares Azzouni (JOR) d. Aki Ismasufian Bin Pj Haji Ibrahim (BRU) 6–2 3–6 11–9
Ahmed Al-Hadid (JOR) d. Tony Shim (BRU) 6–0 6–0
Fares Azzouni/Laith Azzouni (JOR) d. Aki Ismasufian Bin Pj Hj Ibrahim/Latif Isa (BRU) 6–4 6–2

Bangladesh defeated Jordan 2–1
Dilip Passia (BAN) d. Fares Azzouni (JOR) 6–0 6–3
Laith Azzouni (JOR) d. Shibu Lal (BAN) 3–6 6–3 6–2
Shibu Lal/Moin-ud-din Walliullah (BAN) d. Fares Azzouni/Laith Azzouni (JOR) 2–6 6–2 6–3

Bahrain defeated Iraq 2–1
Essam-Jaafar Ali Abdul-Aal (BRN) d. Haider Hussain Kadhim (IRQ) 6–1 6–2
Abdul-Latif Ahmed (BRN) d. Saddam Hussain Kadhim (IRQ) 6–1 2–6 6–2
Saddan Hussain Kadhim/Hussein Ahmed Rashid (IRQ) d. Mohamed Jasim Sanad Ahmed/Essam-Jaafar Ali Abdul-Aal (BRN) 7–6(2) 6–7(3) 7–5

UAE defeated Brunei 2–1
Aki Ismasufian Bin Pj Haji Ibrahim (BRU) d. Mohammed Jamal Buschager (UAE) 6–3 6–2
Mahmoud Nader Al-Baloushi (UAE) d. Chua Pheng How (BRU) 6–0 7–5
Mahmoud Nader Al-Baloushi/Mohammed-Saeed Al-Marri (UAE) d. Aki Ismasufian Bin Pj Haji Ibrahim/Latif Isa (BRU) 7–5 7–6(6)

Jordan defeated Oman 2–1
Mudrik-Nadhim Al-Rawahi (OMA) d. Ahmed Al-Hadid (JOR) 6–1 6–2
Laith Azzouni (JOR) d. Khalid Al-Nabhani (OMA) 6–1 6–4
Fares Azzouni/Laith Azzouni (JOR) d. Khalid Al-Nabhani/Mudrik-Nadhim Al-Rawahi (OMA) 6–4 6–0

Bahrain defeated Brunei 3–0
Essam-Jaafar Ali Abdul-Aal (BRN) d. Chua Pheng How (BRU) 6–0 6–0
Abdul-Latif Ahmed (BRN) d. Tony Shim (BRU) 6–0 6–0
Bader-Jaafar Ali Abdul-Aal/Mohamed Jasim Sanad Ahmed (BRN) d. Aki Ismasufian Bin Pj Haji Ibrahim/Latif Isa (BRU) 7–6(4) 7–5

Iraq defeated UAE 3–0
Mohamad Ibrahim (IRQ) d. Mahmoud Nader Al-Baloushi (UAE) 6–1 6–1
Saddam Hussain Kadhim (IRQ) d. Othman Al-Ulama (UAE) 6–0 6–2
Saddam Hussain Kadhim/Husein Ahmed Rashid (IRQ) d. Al-Ulama/Mohammed Jamal Buschager (UAE) 6–1 6–0

Bangladesh defeated Brunei 3–0
Dilip Passia (BAN) d. Aki Ismasufian Bin Pj Haji Ibrahim (BRU) 6–4 6–4
Shibu Lal (BAN) d. Chua Pheng How (BRU) 6–0 6–0
Shibu Lal/Moin-ud-din Walliullah (BAN) d. Chua Phen How/Latif Isa (BRU) 6–4 6–0

Iraq defeated Oman 2–1
Husein Ahmed Rashid (IRQ) d. Barkat-Salim Al-Sharji (OMA) 6–0 6–0
Mudrik-Nadhim Al-Rawahi (OMA) d. Mohamed Ibrahim (IRQ) 6–4 6–4
Saddam Hussain Kadhim/Husein Ahmed Rashid (IRQ) d. Khalid Al-Nabhani/Mudrik-Nadhim Al-Rawahi (OMA) 7–5 7–5

Jordan defeated UAE 3–0
Ahmed Al-Hadid (JOR) d. Mahmoud Nader Al-Baloushi (UAE) 6–7(2) 6–2 6–1
Laith Azzouni (JOR) d. Othman Al-Ulama (UAE) 6–0 6–1
Fares Azzouni/Laith Azzouni (JOR) d. Mahmoud Nader Al-Baloushi/Mohammed-Saeed Al-Marri (UAE) 6–4 6–3

Bangladesh defeated Iraq 3–0
Dilip Passia (BAN) d. Mohamed Ibrahim (IRQ) 1–6 6–3 6–2
Shibu Lal (BAN) d. Saddam Hussain Kadhim (IRQ) 6–3 1–6 6–4
Muammer Husain Khan/Moin-uid-din Walliullah (BAN) d. Haider Hussain Kadhim/Husein Ahmed Rashid (IRQ) 6–2 2–6 6–2

Bahrain defeated Jordan 2–1
Essam-Jaafar Ali Abdul-Aal (BRN) d. Ahmed Al-Hadid (JOR) 6–1 6–1
Laith Azzouni (JOR) d. Abdul-Latif Ahmed (BRN) 6–4 6–4
Essam-Jaafar Ali Abdul-Aal/Mohamed Jasim Sanad Ahmed (BRN) d. Fares Azzouni/Laith Azzouni (JOR) 6–2 6–3

Oman defeated Brunei 2–1
Mudrik-Nadhim Al-Rawahi (OMA) d. Latif Isa (BRU) 6–1 6–0
Khalid Al-Nabhani (OMA) d. Aki Ismasufian Bin Pj Haji Ibrahim (BRU) 6–2 6–2
Aki Ismasufian Bin Pj Haji Ibrahim/Latif Isa (BRU) d. Khalid Al-Nabhani/Mudrik-Nadhim Al-Rawahi (OMA) 7–6(3) 7–5

Bahrain defeated Bangladesh 2–1
Essam-Jaafar Ali Abdul-Aal (BRN) d. Muammer Husain Khan (BAN) 6–3 6–2
Dilip Passia (BAN) d. Abdul-Latif Ahmed (BRN) 1–6 6–3 6–4
Essam-Jaafar Ali Abdul-Aal/Mohamed Jasim Sanad Ahmed (BRN) d. Muammer Hussain Khan/Moin-ud-din Walliullah (BAN) 3–6 6–3 6–3

Iraq defeated Jordan 3–0
Husein Ahmed Rashid (IRQ) d. Fares Azzouni (JOR) 2–6 6–3 7–5
Saddam Hussain Kadhim (IRQ) d. Ahmed Al-Hadid (JOR) 6–2 7–5
Haider Hussain Kadhim/Husein Ahmed Rashid (IRQ) d. Laith Azzouni/Yazid Saoud Ahmad Nsairat (JOR) 1–2 (40–0) ret.

Oman defeated UAE 2–1
Mudrik-Nadhim Al-Rawahi (OMA) d. Mahmoud Nader Al-Baloushi (UAE) 6–3 6–2
Othman Al-Ulama (UAE) d. Khalid Al-Nabhani (OMA) 6–1 6–3
Khalid Al-Nabhani/Mudrik-Nadhim Al-Rawahi (OMA) d. Mahmoud Nader Al-Baloushi/Othman Al-Ulama (UAE) 7–5 6–7(5) 3–2 ret.

The second time is not necessarily easier, but a number of helpful and insightful people inside and outside my business made it possible. A hearty thank you to Neil Amdur, Jonas Arnesen, Peter Berlin, Philippe Bouin, Paul Chingoka, Gianni Clerici, Alain Deflassieux, Jan Francke and the Swedish Tennis Association, Jane Fraser, Neale Fraser, Margaret Heenan, Bjorn Hellberg, Alun James, Janette Kvasnicova and the Slovak Tennis Federation, Paolo Leonardi, Philippe Maria, Harry Marmion and the United States Tennis Association, Vincenzo Martucci, Nicola Pietrangeli, the Royal Belgian Tennis Federation, Federica Scalabrino, Ubaldo Scanagatta, Christopher Stokes, Brian Tobin, Rino Tommasi, Alan Trengove, Randy Walker, and Kelly Wolf. A special thanks to Linda Pearce in Melbourne for her input.

Let me express particular gratitude to the following players, captains, and coaches who shared their time and thoughts privately: Boris Becker, Paolo Bertolucci, Jonas Bjorkman, Byron Black, Wayne Black, Alex Corretja, Andrea Gaudenzi, Tom Gullikson, Magnus Gustafsson, Carl-Axel Hageskog, Anders Jarryd, Jan Kroslak, Karol Kucera, Nicklas Kulti, Magnus Larsson, Todd Martin, Miloslav Mecir, Carlos Moya, John Newcombe, Yannick Noah, Magnus Norman, Larri Passos, Patrick Rafter, Tony Roche, Marc Rosset, Marat Safin, Jorge Salkeld, Manuel Santana, Gavin Siney, Mikael Tillstrom, and Christophe van Garsse.

An elaborate tip of the hat to Barbara Travers, dashing designer Derek Ungless, and Alexandra Tart at Universe for their patience and professionalism. Finally, a deep bow in the direction of my wife and my parents, who provided moral support and more throughout this bustling, fascinating year.

Christopher Clarey